Scriptures for the Church Seasons

Lent 2013

Following the Way

MARK PRICE

A Lenten Study Based on the Revised Common Lectionary

Abingdon Press / Nashville

FOLLOWING THE WAY
by Mark Price
A Lenten Study Based on the Revised Common Lectionary
Copyright © 2012 by Abingdon Press

ISBN-13: 9781426749650

Manufactured in the United States of America

12 13 14 15 16 17 18 19 20 21—10 9 8 7 6 5 4 3 2 1

Contents

Introduction

The winter months have been especially cold and gray. Part of the reason has been the weather, but part of the reason has been my feeling that I have been in the presence of death more frequently than I can ever remember. The chill of the weather and the chill of mortality have intersected and left me shivering into spring.

A couple weekends a month I serve as a chaplain at a large downtown medical center. During my rounds, I may see a cancer patient barely able to rasp out a word or two, a patient in ICU hooked up to so many machines and tubes that she is barely recognizable, or a recent arrival at the psychiatric unit who has tried (and failed) to commit suicide.

Once I sat at the bedside of a man who was barely forty, his face dark, grayish red from renal failure, his thinning hair disheveled from sleepless sleeping. AIDS was taking its toll, and he was wrestling with his fear of approaching death, the unknown, the prospect of pain and more suffering. He asked, "Was it wrong to hasten this terrible specter—death?" He was so tired; he was so afraid. The thought of leaving behind his family and friends was as painful as his desire to seek a drug-induced unconsciousness.

Even as I talked with him, read the Psalms to him, and held his hand in prayer, I felt, well, anguished. It wasn't that I could not speak the words of hope that were needed; it was just that in that moment, with the taste of death so cloying, I felt more apprehensive than confident. The nearness of death seemed more real to me than the nearness of God. And that was chilling.

Last week, I held hands with some friends and prayed over a beloved family member whose body finally gave out and embraced the liberation of death. She passed away in her sleep and was still nestled in the folds of her bedclothes. She looked peaceful. Yet, the look of death, even when it is anticipated and welcomed, is nonetheless disconcerting precisely because it is so final. It is the only thing we know we cannot humanly undo. And so for a moment, in spite of the assuring words I spoke outwardly and the laughter we all shared remembering her life, inwardly I felt a chill.

This winter, I've also been going out to the state's maximum-security prison to study the Bible with inmates. For several weeks, I have walked alone from the razor-wired entrance across the eerily quiet, frigid yard to the chapel building.

My walk takes me by the area reserved for the execution of death row inmates. I don't actually see the area (though I am aware of it); what I do see are the faces of prisoners. The faces of human beings. Like me. Political posturing and capital punishment debates notwithstanding, what struck me most on my long walks across the prison yard was the familiar human experience common to us all: death. Ultimately what a convicted murderer's heinous crime and own death by lethal injection boil down to is death. And the thought of that left me, once again, with a chill.

Reminds me of the disciples in the Gospels. Jesus tries to talk to them several times about his coming death. They don't understand. They're all afraid to mention it. I think I know how they feel. The cold, gray part of life, which is death, is as inevitable as this season of winter. And yet I would just as soon skip right by it. I want to get to spring. Just like I want to get to the Resurrection. The problem is that the journey to spring—and to the Resurrection—travels through the valley of the shadow of death. That's why Jesus kept telling his disciples that he had to die first.

But they didn't want to believe him. And I would have responded the same way; I don't want to hold death's hand, mine or anyone else's. I'm also not crazy about trying to understand Jesus' death either. I also look past the dying Christ because I am too ready to embrace the Christ in his resurrection. Yet the witness of the gospel reminds me that recognizing the Christ who dies and the Christ who is raised is the Christ we are called to follow. The season of Lent is the time to contemplate that and to practice walking in that way. But don't be surprised if along the way you feel a chill. The good news is that the way of Christ is the way of death that leads to life.

To-Do Lists

This week's readings amount to a fine Lenten to-do list. First on the list, from the Deuteronomy passage, is to make an offering. At every stage along the journey to being God's people, acts of grateful, celebratory worship are a must. Open your hands. Next on the list, from the Epistle text, is to make a confession, not in the sense of some admission of guilt but an expression of faith. Open your mouth. Last on the list, from the Gospel story, is to make a stand—a stand in the face of all that hinders our relationship to God. Open your heart.

My school-aged daughter was trying to make a sentence with one of her spelling words. She asked me to help. "What is the word?" I asked. "*Geotropism*," she replied. "Oh . . . right. Let me think." The *geo* prefix was Greek for "earth." I got that. But no such luck with *tropism*. I had to confess my ignorance and suggested we look up the word. *Geotropism* is a form of the biological term *tropism* (from the Greek *trope*, meaning "turning"). The term relates to plants and refers to the tendency for the roots of a seed to turn downward toward the earth regardless of the way in which the seed is planted. This phenomenon is what enables a plant to anchor itself in the soil and grow. If it weren't for geotropism, I'd eat a lot less tomatoes in the summer.

As I began to contemplate this season of Lent, that word *geotropism* came to mind. I believe we are supposed to be much like plant seeds in our spiritual lives. We should operate by the principles of what might be called *theotropism*. That is, a turning toward God. Our spiritual roots should bend toward the source that will nourish our souls so that our stems branch out and bear the fruits of discipleship. Our problem is that unlike a seed or a bulb, we do not respond automatically to stimuli; in fact, we need to generate or locate some of our own sources of stimuli. Let me suggest some stimuli for the weeks ahead. It is a to-do list that will help you turn toward God with gratitude and celebration.

First, make time to pray, remembering that consciously breathing "Lord have mercy" counts as praying. Listen. A breeze, a stream, a storm, a hearthfire, a melody. Since most of us generally talk too much, choose to relinquish your microphone for a few weeks. Read. Read the Bible, of course; the week's lections are the place to start. But also read a poem daily, the words of a favorite writer, or something a loved one wrote to you long ago. Look. Concentrate your gaze on something not on television—a piece of art, an object such as a stone or a thorn, or a cross, a candle flame, a face.

Above all: be quiet. Keep this thought in mind for the weeks ahead: It's from Wendell Berry describing in one of his briefest Sabbath poems the "Best of any song / is bird song / in the quiet, but first / you must have the quiet."[1]

FIRST FRUITS
AND REMEMBERING
DEUTERONOMY 26:1-11

It is not uncommon still to hear some folks remark that they have little use for regular churchgoing since God (they claim) can just as well accept an offering of worship made out in the middle of a mountain lake, in a clearing in a forest, or sitting on the porch at home. This is true. Sort of. From the biblical point of view, what is truer is that there is something uniquely invaluable (and therefore necessary) in the act of worship performed in line with certain stipulations and in a particular place. In fact, the Book of Deuteronomy is a thirty-four-chapter discourse on why that is so.

This discourse takes the form of a great farewell speech. Moses stands "beyond the Jordan, in the land of Moab" (Deuteronomy 1:5) to address the Hebrew people one last time, calling them to remember how they came to be delivered from slavery and deposited right across the shore of a new land; the land is new because it is a place they could actually settle and build homes and grow olives for themselves instead of a Pharaoh. The point of this trip down memory lane was to promote obedience. In order for God's people to remain God's people (safe and sound in a land flowing with milk and honey), they were to be faithful to the rules of this newly formed community both relationally and ritually. They were to love the Lord with all their heart and soul and might, keep the commandments like they were wristbands or headbands, and teach the next generation to do likewise. And to help the people maintain this level of devotion, Yahweh (speaking through Moses) prescribed a course of action characterized by regularly scheduled celebrations and liturgical practices. These celebrations and practices required the people to show up at a specified place at a specified time to perform specified acts in the presence of specified people. In a word, worship.

By Chapter 26, Moses is coming to the end of his speech, and in these first eleven verses, he prescribes a simple liturgy for the people to use at harvest time. Simple to follow but profound in import. Bring a basket of the first pickings, grain, fruit, vegetables, to the central sanctuary and present it to the clergy on duty. Then together, rehearse the story of God's faithfulness to you. Be sure to mention that time your ancestors were enslaved in Egypt and that you'd be lost if it were not for God's gracious generosity. Get on your knees and thank God. Then set up tables, invite your family, your friends, and even those who might be new to the neighborhood, and have a grand feast.

Did you notice what that liturgy entails? First, the offering (verse 2) mandates that the best bounty of the land—the land that was a gift entirely of God's doing—be given back to the Divine Giver in thanksgiving. I can tell you as a longtime tomato grower that it would take great restraint and self-discipline on my part to hold onto that very first ripe red tomato (and pepper and cucumber and squash, you get the point) and save it for some-

thing besides my own table. This particular offering makes clear that neither the soil nor the fruit belongs to the people by right of ownership. Poised to cross the Jordan and settle in the land of Canaan, ending years and years of nomadic life, the people of Israel needed a conspicuous way of reminding themselves that they did not own the land. What better way to do that than having to sacrifice the first and the best of the harvest to a community feast in honor of the Divine Landowner.

Second, the history recital (verses 5-10) makes clear that God's action on Israel's behalf came first. And it came irrespective of any merit on the part of the people. The word translated as "starving" in the Common English Bible translation ("My father was a starving Aramean") and "wandering" in the New Revised Standard translation ("A wandering Aramean was my ancestor")[2] carries the connotation of being lost like straying sheep. God loved them, God delivered them, and God gave them a home. And they were incapable of doing anything to deserve any of it.

Third, the celebration is a community event. It involves sharing the gifts of God with those within the community of faith and those outside it, a tangible, palatable sign of the Creator God's profound generosity. And according to verse 10b, the dinner on the grounds is to begin with a prayer meeting. The kind that requires kneeling and falling on your face.

While the various sections of Deuteronomy were written at different times over an extended period of time, the book was put into its final canonical form after the exile (late sixth or early fifth century B.C.).[3] The reason that it is worth mentioning is that it connects the story of Israel's return to the Promised Land (following the Babylonian Exile) with the story of Israel's entry into the Promised Land (following the Exodus from Egypt). And that is noteworthy because one of the pressing issues that faced the returning exiles was the re-establishment of worship in the Temple, getting back to those tangible practices that defined a group of former brickmakers as God's chosen people. One way to read the Bible's narrative of God and the Hebrew people is as a cautionary tale of what happens when the regular practices of worshiping (and thus obeying) God are neglected or forgotten. Forget to worship and you forget who God is. Forget who God is and you forget who you are and, most importantly, *whose* you are.

The simple practice of worship outlined in this week's text could be a marvelous template for a Lenten discipline. Try this: Make something, grow something, build something with your own hands, take the best part of it (or all of it), and offer it to God in some way. In other words, give it away. And along with that, make a point to reflect on the ways God has led you throughout your life to this moment and get on your knees and thank God for that. Find a way to have that prayer time at the altar in your church's sanctuary or in some other sacred space. Then get out your phone, scroll through your contact list, and invite some folks to dinner to celebrate. Remember to invite someone not in your contact list as well.

What rituals of remembering have been important in your life of faith? What might you offer to God as an expression of your gratitude for what God has done in your life?

NO DISTINCTION
ROMANS 10:8b-13

As I mentioned in my introductory remarks, I regularly lead Bible studies among the inmates at a maximum-security prison. In other words, I often sit among convicted murderers and thieves, all of whom confess with their lips that Jesus is Lord and believe in their hearts that God raised him from the dead. It is one thing to read Paul's words in Romans 10 in the confines of a church classroom with a group of smartly dressed suburbanites who arrived in their own cars from their own homes. It is quite another thing to share that experience with a group of denim-clad felons who arrived in a single-file line from the chow hall on the other side of a prison yard.

During the very first Bible study I led in the prison, I was impressed by the commitment my group of inmates showed for digging into Scripture. Almost all the guys came well prepared. Their Bibles were dog-eared from use and in some places so marked up with colored pencils and pens that I had trouble distinguishing the printed words from their scribbled notes. Their study books were annotated top to bottom, side to side. And consequently, our discussions were rich in insightful conversation and earnest inquiry. A few times as I walked away from the week's meeting across the silent yard to the razor-wired gates, I found myself lamenting how much some of my church study groups lacked in commitment and depth of learning as compared to my prison study group.

Over time, I began to learn the nature of some of my group members' crimes. This happened naturally in the course of our sharing. The information was never solicited; it mostly just came up. But eventually the weight of this knowledge caught me off guard. I found myself less inclined to listen to our conversations without prejudice. I began to see myself in a different category than these men. "For one believes with the heart and so is justified." Really? Even a convicted *fill in the blank*? "The same Lord is Lord of all and is generous to all who call on his name." Really? Even someone who has committed *fill in the blank*? Even this person who I have heard recount his unspeakable crime to the parole board?

My coleader and I were told when we first arrived at the prison to start this Bible study that all we could bring in past the checkpoint was our study materials. So for several weeks we did just that. We shoved our Bibles and books and shoes through the scanner and offered our hands for the mandatory luminescent stamp. Then as we made our way through the stories of the Old Testament, we read about Abraham and Sarah setting out a picnic lunch for three strangers. Jacob feeding his fragile father a savory stew of deception. Moses and the newly delivered Hebrews collecting their daily portion of manna in the wilderness. Joshua and company sharing the first Passover meal in the Promised Land. David eating the bread of the presence. The prophet Elijah fed by ravens. And Isaiah foreseeing the day when all people would share in a banquet on God's holy mountain. God's grace was so often made known in an act of sharing food. I'm not exactly sure when it happened, but at some point not long before we began our study of the New Testament, we brought a plate of muffins to the checkpoint and shoved them through the scanner. And they made it to the other side. Our prison friends ate them with conspicuous relish that night, as they did the brownies the next week and the pecan pie the next week and so on. From then on, we fellow students of the Bible, walking with Jesus as he ate with sinners and Pharisees alike and fed multitudes with less than we had, broke bread together. When we got to the Gospel of Luke, it was getting close to the season of Lent, Fat Tuesday to be exact. You can guess what we shoved through the scanner that night . . . a King Cake (without the little toy baby inside, of course). It was a delicious accompaniment to the story of Jesus and the travelers to Emmaus.

But alas, after that evening, the prison warden got wind of our unauthorized banqueting and our group's study snack was henceforth forbidden. My coleader and I were chagrined and disappointed as we made the walk together across the prison yard the next week. We were sad for ourselves but primarily for our Bible study friends. Yet we understood this was not a church classroom we were walking to. This was a building in a state prison, a place with rules and rooms with bars and men with criminal records.

That night during our break time, the table empty before us, I heard a rustling sound from somewhere in the room that sounded like a plastic bag. Then, from beneath his chair, a silver-haired lifer (that is, he will never leave prison because of the nature of his crime) brought out a rectangular box of oatmeal pies. Twelve individually wrapped oatmeal pies, one for each of us around the table. He had purchased them with his own money from wherever in prison an inmate buys such things.

He distributed his gift to each of us, and someone offered a blessing over them. Then we unwrapped them and ate. The lump in my throat was so big I could barely get the smallest bite of my oatmeal pie past it. But we all did eat together and then resumed our study. I learned later that the inmates had heard about the warden's decision to close down our contraband snack operation, and they were much more concerned about our feelings about it that about their loss of a weekly treat. Beats all.

I also learned what Paul meant when he said, "There is no distinction between Jew and Greek" (verse 12). Gathered around a table in a prison sharing an oatmeal pie with murderers and thieves, God's unconditional mercy was acted out for me. Well, no, it was actually offered to me by a fellow sinner, who, like me, confesses with his lips that Jesus is Lord.

What is it like for you when you are with someone very different from you? What feelings or thoughts do you have? How does Romans 10:12 address your experience?

"WHO DO YOU THINK YOU ARE?" LUKE 4:1-13

Psst! Hey, you! How long have you been out here anyway? Nearly forty days, eh? That's quite a while. What on earth have you been doing all that time? Oh, right—fasting and praying.

I suppose that's about all a fellow can do out here. Whose bright idea was it to come out here anyway? Oh, right, God. So all this is some kind of spiritual discipline for you, isn't it? Impressive. It takes quite the stamina to stay out here in this god-forsaken desert, sitting all alone, sleeping on stones, stepping around scorpions. I would never send a kid of mine out here. But who am I to say?

Bet you're hungry. And thirsty. You look pale. Imagine what a nice, hot loaf of bread would taste like right about now. It would melt in your mouth. Why not fix yourself a little something to eat? You've carried this spiritual discipline thing way too far. Come on, do yourself a favor. Look around at your feet; stones are everywhere, and if you squint your eyes, why, they could be loaves of bread. Surely if God brought you out here, God wouldn't want you to starve to death. Come on, pick up one of those stones. Make it bread and eat. Eat! You're the Son of God, aren't you?

And at that, Jesus picked up a stone and hurled it into the blazing sun and said, "People won't live only by bread" (verse 4). Jesus was as good at wielding Scripture as he was at throwing rocks. Not only that, Jesus was the Son of God and he knew it. Dripping with the Jordan, he had heard the voice tell him that already. Jesus knew exactly who he was. So Jesus had to know that he could have fed himself at any moment. But he chose not to.

Funny thing about temptation: it's rarely an invitation to do what we cannot do, but what is well within our power to do. In the desert with nothing to depend on but God, Jesus chose to let stones be stones. Perhaps he took the time then to prepare his "I Am the Bread of Life" speech.

Psst! Hey, it's me again. I want to show you something. [Suddenly the sky shimmered and transformed into a panoramic view of the great power centers of the world.] Take a look at that, will you? Can you believe what all power and wealth can accomplish? Look west. The Romans have established their rule almost everywhere. Look east. What do you think of those palaces? I can deliver all of it into your hands. Really. You can have it, the power to do anything, to possess anything, to become anything.

Because look at you; your clothes are rags and very little is left of your sandals. The heat is cooking your flesh, and the animals are waiting to devour you as soon as you're done. What do you have? Nothing. You are as barren as this wilderness. But look at me. Read my lips: all glory, laud, and honor are yours for the asking. I promise. All I ask is, well, a little respect. Actually, more than that. I will require you to sign here, acknowledging me as Supreme Being.

And at that, Jesus said, "You will worship the Lord your God and serve only him" (verse 8). The lure of worldly power is such a glittering gem to the eye. To be able to speak a word and make things happen. To be able to afford the construction of beautiful dwellings and monuments. To be able to command legions of soldiers or create policies and laws. Wow, who wouldn't consider selling themselves to the devil for all that? Well, Jesus for one. He saw the flaw in the gem. Ultimately, for those who acknowledge the authority of the Creator of the world, there can be no other power. True power and authority is not up for sale. Only the illusion of it is. Buyer beware.

Psst! Hey, one more thing, and I'll leave you alone. Let's take a walk. Up here. Right . . . up here . . . on the top . . . of the Temple. There now. Look down at all those people milling about. What do you think they would do if you were to leap off this pinnacle and land safely on the ground right in front of them, not a mark on you? You would certainly have their attention, wouldn't you? Yes indeed. I think you'd have their allegiance too. And isn't that what you're here for? Don't you want these sheep to follow you? Then give them something spectacular to follow. Give them a show!

Because right now you're not even on their minds. Nothing about you screams, "This way to God!" You've been hanging around that loud-mouthed John the Baptist character and all that got you was a bath in the river. Miracle workers and street preachers are a dime a dozen around here. I can assure you no one is going to buy your claim to be the Son of God unless you show them something that will make their jaws drop. Trust me.

And at that, Jesus turned and walked away. "Don't test the Lord your God," he said (verse 12). Because Jesus knew that trying to test God implied that you really didn't trust God. How could he not

trust the One who named him Beloved? And of course for Jesus to trust God the Father meant to trust himself, the Son. That meant he had no use for spectacle or show. The world's fondness for believing that "you're only as good as your last performance" would prove to be a constant challenge to Jesus' mission, which made it the perfect temptation here at the outset.

Provision. Power. Performance. The three temptations Jesus confronted in the desert encompass virtually the gamut of human desire, essentially to be our own god—self-sufficient, all-powerful, and the center of attention. Good thing Jesus knew who he was at his baptism. We would do well to remember our own baptism when God called us to be beloved sons and daughters, for the devil is sure to return at an opportune time.

What temptations have threatened your relationship with God? How do such temptations threaten how you might use the talents God has given to you?

1. From *A Timbered Choir: The Sabbath Poems 1979–1997*, by Wendell Berry (Counterpoint, 1998); page 207.

2. *New Revised Standard Version of the Bible*, copyright 1989, Division of Christian Education of the National Council of the Churches of Christ in the United States of America. Used by permission. All rights reserved.

3. From *The New Interpreter's Bible*, Vol. II (Abingdon Press, 1998); pages 278–280.

This Ain't Easy

faith → trust

Scriptures for Lent:
The Second Sunday
Genesis 15:1-12, 17-18
Philippians 3:17–4:1
Luke 13:31-35

Being God's people has never been particularly easy. The Bible attests to that beginning in the garden of Eden. Closer to home, here in the twenty-first century in a country with abundant resources, great power, and assurances of self-sufficiency posted on billboards everywhere, being Christian is still no piece of cake but for slightly different reasons.

The problem for Abraham in Genesis 15 had to do with biology and logistics. He and his wife Sarah were both sporting barren bodies and, having left behind their home, were caravanning with a fleet of family and livestock across a barren desert. Where was this descendent God had promised? How were a bunch of nomads going to settle in an unknown land? When things on the ground look bleak, it ain't easy lifting your eyes to the night sky. Trusting God is hard.

Paul's concern (big enough to cause him "deep sadness") in writing to the Philippians was how to transform enemies of the cross into imitators of Christ (3:18). The very notion of copying the life and character of another is problematic in and of itself, even when the exemplar in this case is not Christ but Paul the apostle. But evidently self-indulgence is as much a barrier to faithful following as anything. Even imitating a fellow imitator of Christ is hard.

By Luke 13, Herod isn't the only one who wants Jesus out of the picture. But now some of the Pharisees, not exactly Jesus' big fans, make it a point to inform Jesus that he is putting his life on the line. Jesus' response is to confirm their assessment of his mission. His ministry of healing and exorcizing has been a necessarily risky venture. Being God is really hard.

Trusting God is still hard. But the problem for us can be overabundance as much or more than barrenness. The imitation of Christ or Paul, or any other Christian for that matter, is still hard because it gets easier and easier these days to live as enemies of the cross. As you read and reflect on this Sunday's Scriptures, consider spending some time this Lent with the devotional classic *The Imitation of Christ* by Thomas à Kempis.[1]

JUSTIFICATION BY TRUST
GENESIS 15:1-12, 17-18

Being a parent is, I think, one of the greatest tests of faith there can be. Not too many months after our first child was born, my wife and I decided to take her to church. Only it was not Sunday. No service was scheduled. The sanctuary was empty. That was what we wanted. Just us, Kathryn, and God. I cannot recall the exact shape of our prayer or the words we spoke; I know only that we made a point to thank God for the gift of our child and to pledge to be faithful stewards of her life. We gave audible and visible utterance of our trust in God's gracious care of our daughter and in God's gracious guidance of us as new parents. Then we walked out of that sacred space and into the world.

During the next two decades, we loved, fed, clothed, bathed, rocked, taught, prayed for, restrained, scolded, loved, driven, upbraided, goaded, financed, counseled, humored, lost, found, cried over, laughed with, picked up after, let go, welcomed back, and loved our daughter (and our son, too).

Throughout that journey, again and again I have found myself wondering, "God, are you here? Why don't you show up?"

Before I really knew what I was doing, I signed up with God. I committed to follow this God who, I was informed, had created me, had a place for me in the world, and had promised to be with me. I have maintained that course, albeit somewhat unevenly, for quite a while. Some years into being a parent, however, I was startled to realize that trusting God was not going to be so simple. I was seeing evidence that made me question whether God was relevant or even present.

In Genesis 15:4, we have the one of three promises to Abraham that he and Sarah will have a son (see Genesis 17:15-19 and 18:9-15 for the other instances) and become ancestors of many nations. The first time, Abram (he has not been renamed yet) squints up at God with a doubtful expression on his face and asks for some clarification: "We still have no son; exactly how can you keep your promise to us?" The second time, God elaborates on the plan for land and progeny, and Abraham laughs out loud: "You've got be kidding! After all this time? We're old and as barren as the desert." Then the third time, God drops by to remind them of the promise, and Sarah decides to listen in and ends up being the one to laugh. Abram in Genesis 15 is clearly "reckoned as righteous" by God because he trusts God at God's word. But God's word is slow in coming to pass. And the promise itself seems far-fetched. What are we to make of this? The Old Testament scholar Walter Brueggemann offers this insight:

> Abraham and Sarah were called out of their barrenness (11:30) by God's powerful word (12:1). Their pilgrimage of hope had begun on no other basis than the promise of Yahweh (12:1-4a). The *promise* of Yahweh stood over against the *barrenness*. But when we arrive at chapter 15, the barrenness persists. That barrenness . . . poses the issue for this chapter. . . . It is part of the destiny of our common faith that those who believe the promise and hope against barrenness nevertheless must live with the barrenness. Why and how does one continue to trust solely in the promise when the evidence against the promise is all around? . . .
>
> But finally the new reality of faith for Abraham must be accounted as a miracle from God. The faith of Abraham should not be understood in romantic fashion as an achievement or as a moral decision. . . . He did not move from protest (vv. 2-3) to confession (v. 6) by knowledge or by persuasion but by the power of God who reveals and causes his revelation to be accepted. . . . The text announces afresh what it means to be the human creatures we are created to be, that is, to be righteous. It means to trust God's future and to live assured of that future even in the deathly present.[2]

"To trust God's future . . . even in the deathly present." Sounds right, but that is so hard to do. Even Abraham, some time after that moment of clarity out under the night sky counting the endless stars, couldn't help but laugh at the whole wild notion of being a father.

I worry for my children's future as any parent does. But as a parent who has claimed God's promise, I also trust their future to that promise. And then I get another eyeful of the deathly present, and I doubt and worry some more. And I am afraid. I imagine I am not alone in that feeling. Let me make a suggestion then, to those of you who can relate. I like God's opening speech to Abram in Genesis 15:1 in the New International Version. Read it aloud: "Do not be afraid, Abram. I am your shield, your very great reward."[3] Read it over again until you can grasp the meaning of the images. Shield and reward. God is out in front of us always guarding and, all the while, behind us always giving.

But how can I be sure? I cannot help but worry and at times even despair for my children and myself. What can I do? What can anyone do? Maybe we need to go outside tonight and take God's command as addressed to us: "Look up at the sky and count the stars" (verse 5). Might be a good Lenten practice this season.

When has it been difficult for you to trust God? What thoughts and feelings emerged during that time? How was God present for you?

HEY, LOOK AT ME!
PHILIPPIANS 3:17–4:1

Suit the action to the word, the word to the action, with this special observance, that you o'erstep not the modesty of nature. For anything so o'erdone is from the purpose of playing, whose end, both at the first and now, was and is, to hold, as 'twere, the mirror up to nature.

Hamlet, Act 3, Scene 2[4]

Like Paul in the third chapter of his letter to the Philippians, Shakespeare's Hamlet is giving instructions in the art of imitation. Hamlet's words articulate a basic axiom of drama: The most effective acting is the kind that enables the audience to see a representation of the truth. Hamlet's point is that exaggeration ends in caricature and imitation ends in character identification. Hamlet wants the actors in the "play within a play" to make his uncle Claudius "see" himself revealed as the murderer of Hamlet's father.

Today, unfortunately, whenever we use or hear the word *imitation* we usually attach to it the qualifier *cheap* and think of something as fake or false or of lower quality. The Greek term *mimesis*, the origin of our English word *imitation*, does not carry that connotation of cheapness. Instead it suggests the representation of another's actions and motivations in order to convey a particular truth of character. And that is just the word Paul uses to start his sentence in Philippians

3:17: "Brothers and sisters, become imitators of me." Actually, the word Paul uses is *symmimētēs*, which includes the prefix *sym* to mean literally "imitate together." His instruction to the Philippian Christians is for them *to represent themselves* as Christ's followers and use him (and others like him whom they know) as their templates. In other words, to be a community that displays the character of Jesus, be good imitators of good imitators of Christ.

If that sounds a bit strange or confusing, consider this: What is your typical response when you hear someone mention Mother Teresa, Gandhi, Oscar Romero, or Martin Luther King, Jr. as an "exemplar" of faith, courage, sacrifice, or well, anything? You shake your head and admit that the bar set by those kinds of people is set way too high for you to ever reach. They inspire us, yes, but they seem beyond our capacity to imitate. And then we recall Paul telling those Christians over in Ephesus, "Therefore, imitate God" (Ephesians 5:1). We cringe and think, *You've got to be kidding. Really?*

Back to Paul. "Be united in imitating me," he says to the Philippians in 3:17 (New Jerusalem Bible).[5] "You became imitators of us," he reminds the Thessalonians (1 Thessalonians 1:6; NRSV). Why him? Why not him? Remember, he is the guy who got knocked off his high horse when he thought he was doing the right thing persecuting Jesus' followers. He's the guy who can't stop talking about how he is chief among sinners. He's the guy with that distracting thorn in his flesh. He's the guy who ends up in jeopardy or jail a few times for being a theological nuisance. Oh, and he's the guy who makes tents on the side to cover his travel expenses. In short, in Paul's own mind he's no saint, no hero. He's just a guy, a well-educated Pharisee guy, of course; but a regular guy nonetheless convinced he is nothing without Christ, a sinner saved by grace through faith.

And who are we? Not perfect by any means and much more likely to identify with a sinner struggling to be a follower than a saint who is so far ahead of us that we can't make him or her out. Perhaps we can be imitators of Paul. We should. And we should look for others like him who are nearby.

Once upon a time in the small town of Hartselle, Alabama, there lived a little old lady everyone knew as Miss Annie Ruth. The last time I was in her home, her rail-thin arm was crooked beneath wisps of silvery hair to prop up her head. Her face and neck were wrinkles upon wrinkles. Her eyes sparkled from the inside out. When she spoke, her voice wavered and crackled like a vinyl record on an old phonograph. Miss Annie Ruth was close to a hundred years young that last time I sat with her in one of her dim living room's ancient chairs. Over the drone of a floor fan she asked me if I have heard the story of the origin of the word *okay*. I had. But I listened again, not because I have to, but because I wanted to. Because the sweet sound of Miss Annie Ruth's trembling speech was like a reassuring caress. Because I glimpsed in her tiny bright eyes something indescribably important that I wish I had in mine. Because her stories held me and connected me to her in a way I didn't often experience. And because we know this story will lead to another, perhaps to the telling of the myth of Narcissus, or to the recitation of a poem, and then to another, and to another . . .

Miss Annie Ruth would tell you that her life's purpose had always been to help children know and appreciate the beauty in the world. Our own children have books of poetry and myth and fable and story given to them by Miss Annie Ruth because she believed there is great beauty in well-written words. Decades ago she published a book of her own poems. Countless children through the years in Hartselle have learned to play the piano from Miss Annie Ruth because she believed there is great beauty in well-performed music. There are four magnificent magnolia trees blanketed in luscious ivy standing in front of Miss Annie Ruth's dilapidated old house because she believed there is great beauty in taking care of the things God has made. The last time I saw Miss Annie Ruth was in the nursing home where she waited in a bed by a window. Not waiting to go home or to die, but waiting for visitors to come by. She was always ready to tell stories to the nurses who came to change her clothes and her sheets and to perform those daily tasks with eagerness not because they looked forward to the chores, but because they looked forward to being with Miss Annie Ruth. Miss Annie Ruth is one of those people Paul would want us to imitate because she lived a life fully and unashamedly illuminated by the light of Christ.

Have you ever known anyone like Miss Annie Ruth? Someone you wanted to imitate? Who? What about them inspired you to want to imitate them?

THE FOX AND THE HEN
LUKE 13:31-35

The tension in the passage is vividly symbolized in Jesus' references to two animals. On the one hand is the fox. This cunning little sneak thief of a predator prowls about, threatening death. On the other hand is the hen, a feathery mother gathering chicks under her wings, the epitome of care and security. Herod is the fox, and Jesus is the hen. The two are not so much enemies as foils to each other's purposes. Power relentlessly stalks what is weak and powerless, seeking to win and control. Love tenderly draws to it what is weak and vulnerable, seeking to provide shelter and security. Jesus thumbs his nose to the agent of power as defined by Herod (the fox) and positions himself as the agent of God's redeeming grace, the hen with wings outstretched.

Lent is the appropriate season to call attention (as Jesus did) to the dangers that lurk too near us, clever and insidious and designed to devour. We overlook them at our peril. But we also concede to them too much influence. Consider the world's Herods, those people or practices that undermine, dismiss, or kill our spiritual impulses for bringing hope, offering healing, extending hospitality, and working for peace and justice. At the same time, we must look to Jesus as our model for staying the course: "Look, I'm throwing out demons and healing people today and tomorrow, and on the third day I will complete my work" (verse 32). Jesus remained unwavering in his work of making the blind see and the lame walk, proclaiming the kingdom of God right in the face of imminent danger. What he understood was that no risk, however powerful, could ultimately defeat God's purpose of redemption. His lament over Jerusalem should be seen as much as anything as a call to repentance. If we find our gaze is turned more toward Herod, we need to turn back. In short, are we with Jesus or not?

In January of 2007, the French government finally got around to honoring officially the village of Le Chambon-sur-Lignon for its role in saving the lives of thousands of Jews from the Nazis during World War II. This little village located in south central France is the only community (as opposed to an individual) to be named by Yad Vashem (The Holocaust Martyrs' and Heroes' Remembrance Authority) as a member of The Righteous Among The Nations, gentiles who rescued Jews from Nazi persecution. I stumbled upon the amazing story of this village in a book a friend gave me some years ago, *Lest Innocent Blood Be Shed: The Story of the Village of Le Chambon and How Goodness Happened There* by Philip P. Hallie. Briefly, during the four years (1940–1944) of the Nazi Occupation of France, the people of Le Chambon took in and protected some five thousand Jewish refugees, many of them children. Some remained with the villagers for the duration of the war, and others were helped to escape into Switzerland. Most remarkable, according to the book's account, is the fact that the Germans and the cooperating French Government in Vichy were aware of what was going on; even the Gestapo knew. Yet somehow the village was left to do its works of hospitality while all around it the dealers of death and destruction were doing their works of horrific evil. The book's author struggles to make sense of it. He speculates that the villagers' quietly persistent nonviolence was key to its being overlooked or tolerated for so long. After the book is published, Hallie comes to believe what happened at Le Chambon was a miracle, writing:

And so I have come to believe that if a miracle is a marvelous event involving spiritual power at its vital center, the efficacy and the survival of the village were miraculous. Whether God used Trocmé and his fellow villagers as instruments, and whether God protected the village from destruction, I leave up to the theologians. But a belief in God certainly motivated Trocmé and the villagers, and the love the villagers displayed was indeed effective.[6]

Miracle, yes indeed, but I see something else, something about that village pastor, André Trocmé. Hallie's book was developed almost entirely from interviews, many he made with Trocmé's wife, Magda. She was, by her own admission, "not a good Christian at all."[7] But she believed her husband was. So does Hallie:

Her husband's ethic drew its power from the life and death of Jesus. The example and the words of Jesus inspired awe in André Trocmé, and he did what he did because he wanted to be *with* Jesus, in the sense of imitating Jesus's example and obeying his words. . . . He wanted to be close to Jesus, a loving disciple who put his feet in Jesus's footprints with stubborn devotion.[8]

Trocmé wanted to be with Jesus, Jesus the hen safely gathering his chicks right under the nose of the fox. Perhaps in his sermons and Bible studies with his parishioners,

Trocmé effectively taught that Jesus was always sticking his neck out for the least, the weak, the vulnerable, and the oppressed. Jesus was the harbinger of a regime not based on violence and hate but on peace and love. The people of Le Chambon took Trocmé, and Jesus, at his life and the result was a story of salvation.

What does the image of the mother hen say to you about God?

1. Available at the Christian Classics Ethereal Library site: *http://www.ccel.org/ccel/kempis/imitation.html.*

2. From *Genesis*, in the series Interpretation: A Bible Commentary for Teaching and Preaching, by Walter Brueggemann (John Knox Press, 1982); pages 140, 145.

3. Scripture quotations marked (NIV) are taken from the Holy Bible, New International Version®, NIV®. Copyright © 1973, 1978, 1984, 2011 by Biblica, Inc.TM Used by permission of Zondervan. All rights reserved worldwide. www.zondervan.com. The "NIV" and "New International Version" are trademarks registered in the United States Patent and Trademark Office by Biblica, Inc.™

4. From *Hamlet* in *The Complete Signet Classic Shakespeare* (Harcourt Brace Jovanovich, 1972); page 937.

5. Excerpt from THE NEW JERUSALEM BIBLE, copyright © 1985 by Darton, Longman & Todd, Ltd. and Doubleday, a division of Random House, Inc. Reprinted by Permission.

6. From *Lest Innocent Blood Be Shed: The Story of the Village of Le Chambon and How Goodness Happened There*, by Philip P. Hallie (Harper-Perennial, 1979); page xxi.

7. From *Lest Innocent Blood Be Shed: The Story of the Village of Le Chambon and How Goodness Happened There* (Hallie); page 152.

8. From *Lest Innocent Blood Be Shed: The Story of the Village of Le Chambon and How Goodness Happened There* (Hallie); page 161.

Self-Exam

Scriptures for Lent: The Third Sunday

Isaiah 55:1-9 - *brace*
1 Corinthians 10:1-13
Luke 13:1-9 - *Devo*

One thing all of today's Scripture texts have in common is a call for self-examination. The prophet Isaiah pleads with Israel to recognize her neediness for Yahweh and her misplaced desire for expending resources for what she doesn't need and then "return to the LORD" (Isaiah 55:7). The apostle Paul encourages the Corinthian congregation to remember the Israelites, both in terms of how God was present with them and in terms of how they turned their backs on God and became idolaters. His hope is that institutional memory will prompt present awareness. Jesus, in telling his parable of the fig tree, makes clear that opportunities for repentance, examining oneself and turning God-ward, are God's gracious gifts. At some point, though, the gift registry will expire.

This theme of self-examination reminds me of a Lent some years ago where I tried to practice some of the spiritual exercise set forth by St. Ignatius of Loyola. Ignatius' original intention was for a person to retreat for a thirty-day period of solitude and self-review in order to deepen the spiritual life. Key to Ignatius' process is an emphasis on the ordered integration of prayer, discernment, and contemplation. I found especially helpful his "General Examen of Conscience." Here are the five points of the exercise "Method for Making the General Examen" (my paraphrase):

First: Thank God for the many blessings and benefits we have received. Second: Ask God for the grace to know our sins and shed them. Third: Request from God a spiritual spreadsheet beginning from the hour that we woke up to the present moment (hour-by-hour, minute-by-minute if necessary) to determine what thoughts, words, and acts need careful examination. Fourth: Ask God for mercy and forgiveness. Fifth: Resolve to repent and make amends with the aid of God's grace. Pray the Lord's Prayer.[1]

Thoughts. Words. Acts. An honest accounting of those should give us pause. How often are our thoughts not God's? How often do our words betray little of where our faith lies? How often do our acts give us away as idolaters? Better start exercising.

DIVINE HOSPITALITY
ISAIAH 55:1-9

John 7:36

One way to understand the Isaiah text for this week is as a divine dinner invitation. Only this time the guest list is made up of folks who got kicked out of the last place they had been invited to. Reminds me of one Christmas morning. . . .

My family and I were living in Louisville while I was in school. Because we were so far from the homes of our extended families, we had planned to have our own holiday meal. We had invited just a few friends. Leonard was a Vietnam vet with a bad case of asthma. He wheezed a lot but somehow managed to make a little money to give to his daughters for school. Daryl was just a kid; at 21 he'd already done about everything illegal a person could do and then some, but the one thing he couldn't do was go home.

Red was a tall, lanky, gruff-looking character named after the color of his scraggly hair and beard. He lived in whatever abandoned building suited him at the moment and liked it that way. J.R. was a skinny, freckled-face alco-holic who couldn't hold a job or stay out of rehab. Shawn was a recovering drug addict who'd been orphaned at the age of five. Phillip, weighing in at 250 lbs, was a forty-year-old blind man who functioned with the mind of a twelve-year-old, but he was the only one of the group with a permanent address. All the others lived in a shelter of some kind (or as in Red's case, actually on the street). I picked them all up on the street corner that Christmas morning.

We crammed ourselves into my little Toyota (windows rolled down) and made our way home. When my two-year-old saw us spill out into the driveway, her eyes were as big as MoonPies. But by the time the table was set and the food was ready to be served, she had become the center of attention. She had Daryl coloring with her on the floor, Leonard was holding one of her toys for her, and J.R. was working on something for her with clay. When it was time to eat, we crowded around our table and held hands for the blessing; and it was a blessing because Red, who never made how his feelings about black people a secret, was holding Leonard's ebony hand. We filed through the kitchen and filled our plates with hot Christmas food. The men ate everything in sight. Phillip ate everything twice. And we all talked and laughed and drank sweet tea and took some pictures. Like families do.

When the meal was finished, some went to watch a ball game. The rest of us lingered around the table until it was cleared. Then we played a game. And what was so amazing about playing was not that we all enjoyed the game, but that while we were playing our differences vanished; our socio-economic status, our various states of mental and physical health, our clothes, our haircuts, our pasts didn't matter for the moment. Around our table of food we were all God's children. And we were all fed in more ways than one.

The words proclaimed in Chapter 55 are addressed to the exiles living in captivity in Babylon. The language is full of imperatives. *Come, eat, listen, enjoy, look, call.* The God of Israel is issuing an invitation to a people long denied a place at a decent table, an invitation to enjoy a home-cooked meal of unimaginable proportions. Yes, these are the same people who could not behave properly the last time they ate at God's table. These are people living in a land where they are not welcomed. They are only tolerated, used for what benefit they can bring to their oppressors. These are people who are now homeless, some barely surviving, some starving to death, some eking out a meager living, some blind, many convinced they are without hope and beyond saving. These are people who vaguely recall a promise of steadfast love made to them (or at least their ancestors) by the God of Abra-ham. This invitation seems to say that such a promise is still in effect. The everlasting covenant is still operative. The Lord is still to be found and still has mercy enough for all. Can this be true?

Around my table that Christmas morning, an invitation of divine hospitality was extended to and accepted by six of my community's exiles. And while their bellies were made full, I know that more than that kind of hunger was satisfied because I was similarly nourished not by the turkey and dressing, but by a double helping of grace that is only made known in the breaking of bread among God's children. One of the tensions in Isaiah 55 is that the problem for the exiles (those who have found themselves outside of their rightful home, and relationship, with God) is exclusion and self-delusion.

Captivity in Babylon has caused Israel to have to live excluded from their prescribed practices of community and worship. At the same time, the people have gradually deluded themselves into thinking they might be able to survive on their own apart from the God who first delivered them from Egyptian captivity generations earlier. Apparently they have become accustomed to "labor for that which does not satisfy" (verse 2, NRSV). Sounds familiar, doesn't it?

It took a meal with six exiles for me to recognize that God's invitation to "come to the waters . . . come, buy and eat" was not only issued to Israel and not only issued to the marginalized and outcast in our day, but also to me (verse 1, NRSV). "I will make an everlasting covenant with you," says the Lord (verse 3). So pull up a chair and let's eat.

What memories do you have of special meals or family gatherings? What challenges you or inspires you about the Christmas meal described above?

THE IDOLS OF MARCH
1 CORINTHIANS 10:1-13

This is an appropriate but troubling text for Christians attempting to accomplish their Lenten to-do list. Paul's purpose in this passage (according to his summary statement in verse 14) is to get the members of the Corinthian congregation to avoid idolatry at all costs. What is troubling, I think, is that today this language of "idolatry" sounds so archaic. When we hear it, we wonder what could be a contemporary expression of an ancient carving on a pole, something we figuratively "bow down to" or even sacrifice ourselves for. Could it be professional sports? Could it be the almighty dollar? Could it be the American flag? Well, yes, but simply to seek a parallel in the twenty-first century for something in the first century is to miss the bigger point Paul is making about idolatry.

Certainly part of the issue for the early church (if we take a clue from what Paul writes earlier in

1 Corinthians 8) was how to live as citizens of a society and also respond appropriately to societal practices (for example, eating meat at the neighborhood cookout that had previously been used in a pagan worship ritual) that might undermine their witness as followers of Jesus. By the time Paul gets to this passage in Chapter 10, however, he has the entire sweep of biblical history in view and sees in it the threads that bind together Israel and the church. More is at stake for Paul than simply offending a neighbor by refusing to eat a lamb chop. From the time of their deliverance from slavery in Egypt, God's people were all guided ("under the cloud", verse 1), protected ("went through the sea", verse 1), consecrated ("baptized into Moses", verse 2), and nourished ("the same spiritual food", verse 3) by a faithful God; even though those same people managed to "worship false gods" (verse 7). What Paul has in mind specifically is the golden calf episode in Exodus 32, when the Hebrew people gave up on Moses and God and decided to make out of their own possessions their own idol to worship. Yet take a look at how often the word *all* appears in those first few verses of 1 Corinthians 10. By inference, Paul seems to be including the Corinthian Christians (and now us) in his exposition of the biblical story. He clearly wants the Corinthians to see themselves as recipients of the same blessings Israel enjoyed and also as

subject to the same displeasure by God at their sin. But what sin exactly?

In March 2012, the Mega-Million Dollar Lottery jackpot reached a record-setting 640 million dollars. The media outlets were all awash in the news of this momentous occasion. Lottery ticket sellers were reporting brisk sales. Apparently people who never make lottery ticket purchases were plunking down dollars galore. The interviews of local folks I read almost invariably included the mention of giving some of the winnings to the church. After, of course, a little splurge spending and taking care of the family. One fellow, we'll call him Ernest, confessed he planned to buy three tickets, one for the Father, the Son, and the Holy Spirit. (He did not win, so evidently neither did the Trinity.) These lottery games are present now in almost every state in the Union. In spite of the controversy they still stir up, they have gradually become part of our set of cultural practices. What this record-setting jackpot brought to my attention, though, was one of the basic motivations for people's ticket purchases: freedom from worry. Can it be true that no one takes seriously Jesus' comforting words, "Therefore, I say to you, don't worry about your life, what you will eat, or about your body, what you will wear. There is more to life than food and more to the body than clothing" (Luke 12:22-23)?

Are we that anxious about our lives? Are we so unconvinced of God's providential care that we will put our trust (even if fleeting) in a 1 in 180,000,000 chance at a half a billion dollars?

The impatient Hebrews plunked down what gold they had on the chance that a lifeless statue of a four-legged animal would be a better gamble than the cloud by day (they could see) and the fire by night (they could feel) that had led them out of oppression. The Corinthians were banking on their baptismal assurance and regular communion meals together to cover a multitude of indiscretions both social and sexual. The truth is the world is always too much with us. Or as Paul observes, just as soon as you think you're standing, you're bound to fall (1 Corinthians 10:12).

What sin is it exactly that leads us into the idolatry Paul decries in this week's text? I think the sin is distrust of God. By distrust, I mean an intentional denial of God's gracious care fueled by an undue confidence in one's self-sufficiency. When Paul bellows, "Run away from the worship of false gods," I'm pretty certain he is not calling for the Corinthians merely to shun certain eating habits. He is calling them back to Christ and Christ alone. He is calling them to undivided attentiveness to what God has done in Christ and has always been doing in the history of God's people: delivering them from slavery, slavery to others and slavery to self. He is calling them to put their whole trust in the God who promises, sustains, saves, nourishes, and blesses.

During this season of Lent, forego that lottery ticket purchase (or whatever you tend to trust more than God) and commit to throwing your lot in with God. Everything.

Where does your anxiety about your life come from? How do you think God is present for you in the middle of this anxiety?

GRACE AND MANURE
LUKE 13:1-9

I grow tomatoes in my garden. I grow more than I can eat so I can give some of them away. So to make sure I have plenty of tomatoes to harvest, I bury the seedlings in manure when I plant my crop. I am well acquainted with the goodness of manure, and I appreciate Jesus' parable of the fruitless fig tree. It is clearly a lesson in the value of the patient, intentional nourishing and building up of a less than fertile soil bed. Moreover, the point Jesus is making is that the fruit of our repentance, that is, our turning to God in faith and obedience, is something God is willing to wait for ("one more year", verse 8) and give encouragement for ("give it fertilizer", verse 8) but only for so long ("then you can cut it down", verse 9).

I see two ways to respond to this parable. One way is to focus on the righteousness of God and the inevitable judgment that goes along with it. In Luke 12 (preceding the parable of the fig tree), Jesus told a story of some managers whose master discovers their sorry behavior when he returns home unexpectedly and therefore punishes them accordingly. And recall that troubling comment Jesus made right after telling that story, "Do you think that I have come to bring peace to the earth?" (12:51). Well, in truth, the angels at Jesus' birth did say something about peace on earth. What happened to that? Evidently, Jesus is not about to sugarcoat God's purpose in sending him to herald the coming of the Kingdom. The redemption of the world cannot happen without some fallout because some simply will not stand for it. There is a price to pay for an unrepentant heart. Schedule an EKG now.

Another way to respond to this parable is to focus on the unmerited mercy of God and the patience God shows in extending it to us. In the first place, the very presence of a fig tree in a vineyard tells me about the nature of the owner. While it was not particularly unusual to have fig trees in a vineyard rather than in a fig tree orchard, a fig tree would grow large and apparently pull a good portion of nutrients from out of the surrounding soil. To plant a fig tree where grapes are grown seems to me an intentional act of generosity. Then there is the time frame. The parable describes the fig tree having been barren for at least three years. Surely that means that the tree is a mature tree, one that has been planted for quite a while, perhaps even longer than three years. In any case, the parable's point is that the tree has been around long enough to bear some fruit, which is what the tree was meant to do. How long should it take a thing to do what it was created to do? The acceptance by the owner of the gardener's offer to care for the tree another full growing season virtually shouts overabundant generosity. Moreover, fig trees are not known to be high-maintenance trees. The gardener's willingness to provide the fig tree an extra measure of care, to "dig around it and give it fertilizer," is a further signal of the grace being extended to one unproductive inhabitant of an otherwise thriving vineyard (verse 8). This is just like the grace God extends to us, the kind that waits way past a reasonable amount of time and makes the effort to dig in deep with soiled fingers, pressing, prodding, pleading for us to be what we are created to be. *Grace* is the word, I think. It is there to be received. Jesus recommends it to us with obvious urgency, but we must not miss the incredible gift it is.

In the book *Tell It Slant: A Conversation on the Language of Jesus in His Stories and Prayers*, Eugene Peterson offers another word from this parable worth mentioning, particularly relevant during this season of Lent. Peterson observes that Jesus tells this parable just a few days before he entered Jerusalem to eventually be nailed to a cross; and then, while dying on that very cross, repeats a word he used in telling the parable.

> Jesus' prayer to his Father, "Forgive them," is a verbatim repetition of the gardener's intervention, "Let it alone." The Greek word is *aphes*. In some contexts it means "Hands off. . . . Cool it. . . . Leave it alone. . . ." In other contexts having to do with sin and guilt it means "Forgive . . . Remit. . . ." It is the word used in the prayer Jesus taught us, "Forgive us our sins . . ." (Luke 11:4). Here the contexts of parable and prayer converge. . . . For those of us who are up to our necks in manure, which is to say, up to our necks in forgiveness, it is perhaps important to note that the forgiveness Jesus prayed for us was not preceded by any confession or acknowledgement of wrongdoing by the crucifixion crowd or any of us since. Preemptive forgiveness. Jesus prays that we be forgiven before we have any idea that we even need it, "for they know not what they do." No preconditions. Amazing grace.[2]

This year when I plant my tomatoes, I'll see the manure I use in a new light.

How does Jesus' parable speak to you about God's grace? God's forgiveness? God's nurture?

1. From Christian Classics Ethereal Library, *http://www.ccel.org/ccel/ignatius/exercises.xii.iii.html.*
2. From *Tell It Slant: A Conversation on the Language of Jesus in His Stories and Prayers*, by Eugene H. Peterson (Wm. B. Eerdmans Publishing Co., 2008); page 74.

omecomings

Scriptures for Lent:
The Fourth Sunday
Joshua 5:9-12
2 Corinthians 5:16-21
Luke 15:1-3, 11b-32

I grew up in North Carolina, and both of my grandparents' houses boasted generous front porches with enough room for bench swings, rocking chairs, homemade ice cream, and hound dogs underneath. A front porch can make time stand still on summer evenings and make a swig of Coke from a cold bottle taste like it was meant to taste. A front porch can cause you to throw up a hand to wave at passersby, whether you know them or not.

When my family and I moved to a town just on the outskirts of Washington, D.C., we noticed some of the prevalent features of houses in that area was a deck off the *back* of the house, a patio with privacy fence at the *back* of the house, or a sunroom extending off the *back* of the kitchen. The operative word here, of course, is *back*. So of course, the house we finally moved into had no front porch. It did, however, have a large and welcoming front yard; so we decided to place a picnic table under a little cluster of tall trees out at the corner. That became our front porch; we ate lunch there, set up a lemonade stand there, and kept the wiffleball and bat handy there just in case anyone happened by. We even hung out a hammock. All was right with the world until about a month later when someone "borrowed" our hammock and left just the hooks in the trees.

These memories make me think about hospitality and welcoming and home. If we take our cues from the three Scripture passages for this week, how could we miss that our God is the Great Host whose mission is to set the table, fling open the front door, and stand waiting on the front porch? Joshua and the people of Israel finally make it to the place God assured them would be home, and they share a home-cooked meal to say thanks. Paul's Corinthian letter bursts with the incredible promise that God is already working to bring all creation home, and God's people are invited on the front porch to wave and shout the news. Jesus' parable is nothing if not an engraved invitation for the least and the lost to come home.

Our world desperately needs the Bible's message of what I call "front porch" hospitality. We need more front porches, more hammocks out front, and more people out in them. It's a risk, I know. But we live in a world where taking and hoarding increasingly characterize our regular transactions as fellow human beings. We should live better than that. God promises better than that. What would happen if this Lenten season, we placed ourselves intentionally in front of the world, swinging unashamedly in its face and inviting folks to stop by for some lemonade? Sure, I know there are hammock thieves lurking about because front-yard hammocks or front porches or, for that matter, most genuine expressions of self-giving and welcome are a threat to a selfish, backyard world. But I bet we'll meet some passersby looking for places and signs of welcome. If the hammock gets stolen, chalk it up to the price of hospitality. Not to worry, just look for the hooks still in the trees.

DINNER ON THE GROUNDS
JOSHUA 5:9-12

This passage from Joshua 5 is brief. It comes as the climax of Israel's long journey from a confederation of escaped slaves wandering in the wilderness to a fledgling nation of God-chosen people poised on the banks of the Jordan about to enter and settle a new land. This moment is, for want of a better term, momentous. This moment has been coming since Abraham left Haran. This moment is really the culmination of two journeys. The first was Moses' journey with the Hebrew people from Egypt, across the dry bed of the Red Sea, safely into the desert, and eventually to Mount Sinai where they received the Law and the news that they would be walking a while more. The second journey was with Joshua and mostly the children of the group that left Egypt across the dry bed of the river Jordan and safely to the east of Jericho where they made camp, performed a ritual of belonging (circumcision), celebrated a meal of remembrance (Passover), and looked forward to their mission ahead (battling their way into the Promised Land).

As part of both journeys, a milestone is marked by a meal. A dinner on the grounds of sorts. In the case of Moses and the Sinai folks, the milestone was getting safely across the Red Sea ahead of the Egyptian chariots. In short, God saves. The meal consisted of manna and quail catered daily by Yahweh. In the case of Joshua and the Gilgal folks, the milestone was actually arriving in the land of promise. In short, God provides.

The meal consisted of "food produced in the land: unleavened bread and roasted grain" (Joshua 5:11). While the similarities in these two occasions are quite evident, it's the big difference that grabs my attention. When Joshua and the people sat down on their blankets to share a fellowship meal on the grounds of Canaan, their baskets were full of the bread of earth rather than the bread of heaven. The story says that the manna ceased, just stopped appearing, the moment people started eating their own homemade rolls. Now, why would the One Holy God, who saved the Hebrew people and provided for them for so long, stop catering their meals?

I'm going to guess most congregations have marked a special occasion or a particular milestone (perhaps its founding day) with a meal, say, a potluck or a dinner on the grounds. The congregation I belong to has a springtime strawberry festival every couple of years where we all enjoy big pans of poppy seed chicken casserole and desserts made with strawberries. At one time, when the congregation was just starting out, part of the property was used to grow strawberries; and so the Strawberry Festival began as a celebration of people coming together to be a church. Naturally, a component of the celebration came to include an intentional sharing of the produce of the land, the strawberries. Why would a group of God's people

build a festival around tilling and planting and weeding and watering and harvesting and picking and washing and slicing and finally eating the fruit from a plot of ground just outside the church door? The same reason a group of God's people cut and bundled and dehusked and ground up grain to make flour for the dough to bake into cakes to eat in Gilgal.

Out of a generous storehouse of grace, God offers us salvation, deliverance, provision, and hope. Such offerings are ours without condition, but not without expectation. Some response is required. Praise and thanksgiving, yes of course. And one thing more: To be a living, breathing, daily witness to the God who is saving us, who is delivering us, who is providing for us, and who is our one and only hope. Once formed and settled as a community of God's people, we seek to establish practices and traditions that clarify our identity as God's people, only we congregate as part of a larger community full of other people also sharing in the land of milk and honey. Distinctiveness is a discipline, not a default. Self-sufficiency makes an attractive idol.

We need look no further than the first part of the Book of Deuteronomy to hear the clear warning given to the people ready to enter the land of promise:

> When you eat, get full, build nice houses, and settle down, and when your herds and your flocks are growing

large, your silver and gold are multiplying, and everything you have is thriving, don't become arrogant, forgetting the LORD your God. . . . Don't think to yourself, My own strength and abilities have produced all this prosperity for me. Remember the LORD your God! He's the one who gives you the strength to be prosperous in order to establish the covenant he made with your ancestors—and that's how things stand right now. But if you do, in fact, forget the LORD your God and follow other gods, serving and bowing down to them, I swear to you right now that you will be completely destroyed.

(Deuteronomy 8:12-14, 17-19)

Like so many meals in the Bible, the first dinner *on* and *from* the ground for Israel was less about the what (the food) and more about the who (the God who provides). The suggested table talk was more essential than the menu. "God is great, God is good, let us thank him for our food." Seems so simple when you put it that way.

Where do you find yourself trying to maintain the illusion of self-sufficiency? What kind of offering of thanksgiving to God can you make this Lent?

GOD IS ON YOUR SIDE
2 CORINTHIANS 5:16-21

As I write this a year or so in advance of anyone reading it, the big headline now is the devastating tornados that ripped through the state of Texas, leaving death and debris. A week or so ago, the headline was about another mass shooting. A couple of years ago, I recall reading a headline about the continuing crisis in Japan in the aftermath of a devastating earthquake and tsunami: "Tide of 1,000 Bodies Overwhelms Japan." A photograph of a distraught young girl sitting alone amid the debris accompanied the headline. I felt like speaking to her somehow. But what would I say? She looked completely overwhelmed by her sorrow. Read the paper or surf the news sites on the Internet and you could quickly get the impression that the world is in self-destruction mode. Consider the people in your congregation or workplace; and you might discover several friends whose families are in total meltdown, the tragic news of a young man's suicide, news of an elderly woman's life-threatening stroke, news of a high school senior's fatal car accident, a child diagnosed with leukemia, or you fill in the blank.

Recently, as I made my rounds through the halls of a cancer ward and a psychiatric unit, I was made keeper of the stories of more people overwhelmed, people clinging to the thinnest possible thread of life and mental health. One slurred through a morphine daze about wanting desperately to have more time to see her grandchildren. Another grimaced with pain to speak hopefully about the coming of spring outside the window. One, with eyes shut tightly, told tales of depression and addiction and moral failure and marital discord. Another rambled about her fears and anxieties, some real, most imagined. Then the grey-haired lady with the wide blue eyes tapped on the door frame. Her husband had been dead a year, and she suffers from several forms of dementia. She wanted to say this to me: "I lie in bed and pray and pray and pray, but I still don't know what I'm doing. I know God is somewhere. But where?"

During the season of Lent, we will regularly read Scriptures that highlight Jesus' encounters with particular people, people who seem to be struggling (as we all do) with various physical, emotional, relational, and theological issues. In a way, they all present Jesus with a question: Where is God in all this? And Jesus responds by touching them, talking to them, and teaching them. He offers new legs, new perspective, new water, new eyes, new life, and a new picture of God. All well and good, but what about all these people I know, here and now, who are experiencing very real devastation and despair? Where is God in all this?

Good question. According to Paul, the answer is that in Christ, God is "reconciling the world to himself" (verse 19). What Paul means is that the one who created all that exists is in the process of resolving, putting back into balance, and re-establishing the right order of all that exists. God is at work even now in spite of appearances to the contrary. Moreover, we who follow Christ are recipients of something Paul calls the "ministry of reconciliation" (verse 18). I take this to mean that we have been enlisted as God's agents both to witness to the world that it is being reconciled to God and to participate with God in the work of mending those rips and gashes in the world that so often make the news. Ok then, that certainly sounds like a tall order. Perhaps it does, but God has, for some reason, entrusted this message of reconciliation to us. We are, to use Paul's term, God's ambassadors. The role of an ambassador is to be a representative in residence, meaning an ambassador lives temporarily in one country (kingdom) while actually belonging to another. And the whole point of taking up residence in another country (kingdom) is to promote the mission and benefits of the country (kingdom) to which you belong. To do that rightly takes having a clear vision and understanding of the place you belong. Do we have that as Christians? Paul assures us that, thanks to Christ, the old has passed away and "new things have arrived" (verse 17), which means our vision is different. We can no longer look at our world "from human standards" (former or old standards) (verse 16). We now see things from God's point of view, that is, from God's promise that death and despair and sickness and suffering have all been defeated in Christ's own death and resurrection. This is the vision we are to take to the streets.

The grey-haired lady with the blue eyes got up and guided her walker through the door I held open. We had just finished praying together. She looked up at me with glistening eyes, smiled, and said, "I feel much better now; God is on my side. Right?" I said, smiling back, "Right." God is on her side.

And God is on your side. Come to think of it, just about every encounter Jesus had with people—friends, enemies, insiders, outsiders, poor, rich, lame, whole—was an attempt to drive home that truth. I suppose at first glance a statement like that sounds simplistic. And for some, it may always be so. But I look at it this way: At the root of much of the angst, brokenness, and despair that we all experience in life is the nagging belief that we suffer alone. Not that anyone cares, but that no one is there. Right there. On our side. Follow the story of Jesus in any one of the Gospels and you'll see him as a flesh and blood signboard proclaiming that God is on your side. Even more, God is moving everything over to God's side of the balance sheet. Reconciling.

As you look back on tough times in your life, how do you think God was on your side? How might you be an ambassador for Christ?

RADICAL FATHERHOOD
LUKE 15:1-3, 11-32

I'm always apprehensive whenever I approach one of Jesus' parables with a scalpel to open it up to get a good look at its innards. As I came to understand many years ago while writing a curriculum piece on Jesus' parables, interpreting one of Jesus' parables is more about seeing the full view it presents rather than dissecting it to find one meaning. In the case of Luke 15:11-32, the first thing we need to clear away is our presumption that the prodigal son is the focus of the parable. According to Jesus' opening words, his parable is about a man who had two sons (verse 11).

This is a parable of a loving father awaiting and inviting the homecoming of his two sons. Yet while the story is at once a picture of God's grace and a reminder of our need of it, we tend to keep our gaze on the sons. Just as all of us share in the experience of leaving and coming home, so too we share the experience of distancing ourselves from and then finding our way back to God. We easily identify with one or both of the sons. It seems quite natural for us to see ourselves as either the prodigal, the sinner seeking redemption in the world only to find it in the place he left behind; or the elder brother, the homebody whose works of obedience have become his faith.

Think for a moment: When have you ever left home spiritually? When have you taken your "living" into your own hands and left behind your most familiar traditions and values? When have you found yourself resenting those whose homecomings are dramatic and celebrated? Such is the inevitable rhythm of the spiritual journey. And while I have often remained in that trajectory of thought and self-examination, I would push us forward to see that, in his telling of his parable, Jesus wants us to focus on the father.

So look again. Look at the father. As I saw years ago in the curriculum piece, the father is always at home. The father is blatantly generous, inappropriately giving, and unconditionally compassionate. The father is willing to risk the loss of pride and property and place for his children. The father has the authority to keep us but will always let us go our own way and suffer in our absence. The father's hands are always waiting to welcome us with a warm embrace. The father will throw a party for us whenever we come home because, in the scheme of everything that matters, finding the lost is of utmost importance.

In the summer of 1986, the writer Henri J. M. Nouwen was given an opportunity for a private, unhurried viewing of Rembrandt's famous painting *The Return of the Prodigal Son*, on display since the late 1700's at The Hermitage in St. Petersburg, Russia. The canvas is enormous, eight feet by six feet in size; and Nouwen was able to spend about four hours over a period of two days in the presence of this masterpiece. Out of his experience, he wrote a remarkable book about his own spiritual journey, expressed though his personal and profound reflections on the painting and the parable. Though his encounter with Jesus' parable through the lens of Rembrandt's painting, Nouwen sees our ultimate call as becoming the father in the parable, living out a discipline he calls "spiritual fatherhood."

Moving along our journeys of faith, often the prodigal, at times the begrudging elder, we are continually called to love as the father loved. "His outstretched hands are not begging, grasping, demanding, warning, judging, or condemning. They are hands that only bless, giving all and expecting nothing."[1] Along with receiving the promise of unconditional love, we are also called to become "home" for others, to provide a secure and inviting place, an open and celebrative place, a place ultimately where God is made known. "Unlike a fairy tale, the parable provides no happy ending. Instead, it leaves us face to face with one of life's hardest spiritual choices: to trust or not to trust in God's all-forgiving love."[2] Jesus' parable of the loving father does not leave us with a neat moral to remember and to include in the nice package of morals we already live by.

Rather, we are dealing with a calling, a calling to assess our own spiritual journeys at this moment.

Are we at home with the father? If not, then how do we get there? If we are, then how do we become more like the father to others? At issue in each of these questions is our personal spirituality as well as our communal expressions of faithfulness. We must make the effort to evaluate honestly where we are, even if it means admitting we have nothing left but to slop the pigs. We must be willing to risk our very lives on God's forgiving, graceful love. And we must seek our spiritual home in a place other than in a world alien to the things of God. "The world offers us abundant means and methods by which to squander our 'living.' The world would have us all request and spend our inheritances as soon as possible. Likewise, the church can offer a deceptively comfortable place to be a devoted elder brother. But it can also be the place to be the inviting father."[3] Or as Henri Nouwen puts it:

> Although Rembrandt does not place the father in the physical center of his painting, it is clear that the father is the center of the event the painting portrays. From him comes all the light, to him goes all the attention. Rembrandt, faithful to the parable, intended that our primary attention go to the father before anyone else. . . . Perhaps the most radical statement Jesus ever made is: 'Be compassionate as your Father is compassionate.' . . . The return to the Father is ultimately the challenge to become the Father.[4]

The loving father awaits and invites both sons, and you and I, to homecoming.

How might we be more like the loving father in the parable?

1. From *The Return of the Prodigal Son: A Story of Homecoming*, by Henri J. M. Nouwen (Doubleday, 1992); page 137.

2. From *The Return of the Prodigal Son: A Story of Homecoming* (Nouwen); page 75.

3. Some material appeared in the curriculum piece *Formations: Learner's Study Guide*, by Mark Price (Smyth & Helwys Publishing, Inc., 1996); pages 21–25.

4. From *The Return of the Prodigal Son: A Meditation on Fathers, Brothers, and Sons* by Henri J. M. Nouwen (Doubleday, 1992); pages 114–116.

mazing Love

Scriptures for Lent: The Fifth Sunday
Isaiah 43:16-21
Philippians 3:4b-14
John 12:1-8

The Scripture readings for this fifth Sunday of Lent offer poignant love songs from God and to God, and each one demonstrates the amazing love of God. In Isaiah 43, God sings a love song to Israel. Desiring to know Christ fully in his suffering, death, and resurrection, Paul sings a love song to Jesus his Lord in Philippians 3:4b-14. Seeking to express her great love in the most extravagant way she could, Mary spilled a love song all across Jesus' feet in John 12:1-8. The love of God for us is of such a quality and depth that it can barely be described in words. From the Hebrew *hesed* to the Greek *agape*, from Torah to Gospel, the biblical story sings of God's steadfast devotion and covenant care.

Charles Wesley's great hymn "And Can It Be that I Should Gain" echoes the voices of our Scriptures for this day as it points to God's amazing love. Read aloud the first verse printed below as part of your preparation for this fifth week of Lent. Better yet, locate the hymn and pray or sing a different verse every day during the week ahead.

And can it be that I should gain
An interest in the Savior's blood!
Died he for me? who caused his pain!
For me? who him to death pursued?
Amazing love! How can it be
That thou, my God, shouldst die for me?
Amazing love! How can it be
That thou, my God, shouldst die for me?[1]

A BRAND NEW THING
ISAIAH 43:16-21

A few years ago in preparing to write a series of Bible study lessons on the Book of Isaiah, I found that Chapter 43 was one of the most intriguing. The whole text is basically a hymn of praise to God's relationship to Israel. And what I found of particular significance was how often in that chapter

God's speech uses the first person singular *I*. Read these aloud:

"I have redeemed you" (verse 1).
"I have called you by name" (verse 1).
"I will be with you" (verse 2).
"I am the LORD your God" (verse 3).
"I love you" (verse 4).
"I'll gather you" (verse 5).
"I, I am the LORD" (verse 11).
"I announced, I saved" (verse 12).
"I act" (verse 13).
"I'm doing a new thing" (verse 19).
"I'm making a way" (verse 19).
"I, I am the one" (verse 25).

Every time I read those passages, I am awestruck that they are in the middle of the Book of Isaiah surrounded on all sides by reminders and indictments of a people's faithlessness. Their intended impact is not lost on me. God loves Israel with a depth of love that is not conditioned by Israel's response. God loves Israel not because she deserves that love, but because God chooses to keep God's covenant promise to her. God loves God's people just because; and that message is such a surprise when it turns up here in the speeches of an Old Testament prophet.

Surprising or not, though, this message of God's love is vital for our Lenten journey. "I'm making a way in the desert, / paths in the wilderness," God says to Israel (and to us) in verse 19. If we have been practicing any kind of discipline of withdrawal or retreating

or reflecting these last few weeks, then we should be acquainted with wilderness. Few of us can manage to avoid the desert for too long. Barrenness takes many forms and overtakes us at various times throughout our lives. And it is often during those times that we forget the occasions when we basked in the blessings of God's generosity. We may even forget God's pronouncements of steadfast love. According to the Bible, memory fatigue is a common consequence of an exiled community.

So what are we to make of God's command to the people of Israel, "Don't remember the prior things" (verse 18)? Much of Isaiah is concerned not just with rehearsing but with celebrating God's acts of deliverance in past. Why is this prohibition here? I think the point is that the "new thing" God is doing cannot be compared to what God has done so far. The Exodus from Egypt was just a parade compared to the restoration God has in store for God's people in the near future.

I've only attended one high school class reunion, my twentieth. Driving the several hours back home from that occasion, I spent time mulling over where I had come from, replaying in my mind things done and undone, reliving moments both good and not so good, reviewing people and places that had left their marks on me, and recalling where and with whom I had left pieces of myself. I imagined back to a time when the cares and responsibilities of life seemed less heavy, when anything seemed within reach. At times I became simply overwhelmed by the sadness of it all. I wept over the various losses experienced by my friends: a young child dead in the blink of an eye, a brother mentally disabled, a sister lost to cancer, a family broken apart by divorce. It took a call to my best friend, David, to relieve me of the pain of way too much remembering. I had made the mistake of only rehearsing the past, of allowing my eyes to look only backward in time. Thankfully, I had handy the words of my spiritual mentor, Frederick Buechner. In his essay "A Room Called Remember," he put my experience into perspective:

> One way or another, we are always remembering, of course. There is no escaping it even if we want to, or at least no escaping it for long. . . . In one sense the past is dead and gone, never to be repeated, over and done with, but in another sense, it is of course not done with at all or at least not done with us. . . . Old failures, old hurts. Times too beautiful to tell or too terrible. Memories come at us helter-skelter and unbidden, sometimes so thick and fast that they are more than we can handle in their poignance.[2]

Yes, that was exactly what I had experienced, the power and the pain of reliving my past. Then Buechner reminded me that to believe the story of Scripture is to see that remembering and hope go together. To remember is not only to look back in longing and appreciation of all God has done in your life, but to look forward in celebration of what God has yet to do. Buechner writes:

> Hope stands up to its knees in the past and keeps its eyes on the future. . . . To remember the past is to see that we are here today by grace, that we have survived as a gift. . . . [And] because we remember, we have this high and holy hope: that what he has done, he will continue to do, that what he has begun in us and our world, he will in unimaginable ways bring to fullness and fruition.[3]

Thus says the Lord in Isaiah 43: "I am the Holy One who once upon a time made a way for my people through the sea and across the wilderness. But don't think that I plan simply to do the same thing all over again. I have something even better for my people. Something brand new. Look! Look! It's happening. Don't miss it." Thus says the Lord to us: "I am still the Holy One, and I am still doing new things. Just watch!"

What mighty deeds has God done in your life? What do you imagine God might do next?

GAINS AND LOSSES
PHILIPPIANS 3:4b-14

For many years I had the privilege of being part of the editorial team responsible for the DISCIPLE Bible study program. That program is based on the assumption that if congregations read and study the entire Bible together, cover-to-cover, holding each other accountable in prayer and preparation, they would experience significant growth in faith. I've seen that very thing take place in churches. And I've seen that take place in people's lives. The Bible will change you if mess with it long enough.

My friend Jeff is a good example. He and his wife were fairly new to our church when he signed up for the DISCIPLE study that year. Neither he nor his wife had ever cracked open a Bible more than a few times. Jeff had spent his early years bouncing around military chapels. For him, church life had been a kind of generic tour of duty. At the time of the Bible study, he was the owner of a sports bar in the area that specialized in alligator meat appetizers. He was a very sharp dresser, often wore an impressive black leather jacket, and occasionally rode his motorcycle to church. He and his wife also had a new baby.

Now, Jeff could have remained an average church member, attending Sunday school and occasionally worship when he wasn't barkeeping. But he made the dangerous decision to read the Bible in earnest. Near the end of his study, Jeff called me and asked if he could come in and talk to me. When he arrived, I could tell he was trembling just a bit, obviously nervous. I couldn't imagine what he had to say. Jeff said to me that his study of the Bible with his small group of ten had put him in the position of making a hard choice. He wanted my advice. In brief, Jeff had to come to believe he could no longer be the owner of an establishment that depended primarily on the sale of liquor and be faithful to Jesus. Moreover, his experiences as a bartender, his new awareness of Christ's claim on his life, and what he saw as his gifts as a Christian had led him to consider becoming a minister instead. He had come to share that with me, to thank me for encouraging him to read the Bible, to ask me to pray with him for all the transitions to come, and to guide him in selecting his next steps. You could have knocked me over with a newspaper. Within the year, Jeff and his family had sold the business and relocated, and he was enrolled in seminary.

When I read Paul's impassioned narrative in Philippians 3 about how gaining Christ is worth losing everything, I think of Jeff. As best as I can tell, through his encounter with Scripture, Jeff discovered "the superior value of knowing Christ" (verse 8) and decided that all his other gains were no longer worth keeping. They became distractions for him.

By this week in the Lenten season, we have had plenty of time to contemplate and confess our many sins. Perhaps now is the time to consider the relative value of our many gains such as personal achievements, possessions, American Express cards, health plans, retirement accounts, season tickets, and whatever the world and we hold in high esteem. Those are the things that define us more often than not. They draw us to them. They shape (or perhaps misshape) us in their image. And ultimately they will diminish us and keep us from ever fully knowing Christ and "the power of his resurrection" (verse 10).

A couple of years ago, I went to work one morning only to be informed that I had no more work to do. In the blink of an eye, I became unemployed. Two weeks later, a decade worth of files and books were boxed up in my garage. Three months later, I was sitting in a hospital room waiting for my father to be taken into surgery so I could get back to the assisted living residence and get my mother to an outpatient surgery appointment. I must admit that for some time I was overwhelmed with my real and potential losses. I found myself thinking about the career I had attained, the status I had achieved, the contributions I had made, the insurance coverage I had, the security I had provided my family, once counted as gain, now simply gone. Unlike my friend Jeff, I had not chosen to regard my job and my 401(k) from Paul's perspective, "as sewer trash, so that I might gain Christ and be found in him"

(verses 8-9). But I did take some of my lengthy free time to contemplate what I really valued. Was my job, my career, what defined me? Was having the security of a health/dental/vision plan of ultimate significance? To what extent was my identity connected to my accomplishments? And why was I so afraid of losing things?

"I have lost everything for him," Paul says in verse 8. Paul was a brave fellow. And so is my friend Jeff. Paul wrote so confidently, maybe from his prison cell, to the Philippian church about having a proper perspective on his own gains. And my friend Jeff seemed so certain in navigating a life change midstream and trusting God with the details. It took me many weeks sitting in a quiet house during work hours with a cat for company to study my gain/loss balance sheet and see that I needed to recalibrate. I really do want to know Christ, really I do . . . I think. Do you?

What are the things you value most in life? How does the way you value them compare to the way you value Christ?

ON THE SUBJECT OF FEET
JOHN 12:1-8

The story of Mary anointing Jesus' feet with nard comes at the opening of John 12:1-8, just a chapter before Jesus will anoint his disciples' feet with water. Both acts are described in sacramental terms. Both acts involve a form of self-giving. And both acts point to a truth beyond the mechanics of hands touching feet. And today, as I sit here in the house where I grew up, both acts make me think of my mother.

My mother has been living with a diagnosis of Parkinson's disease for nearly two decades now. For many of those years until fairly recently, she only moved from her chair in her combined living and dining room to go to sleep in her bedroom down the hall. As I sit at our dinner table, I can see hanging over the chair a framed print of William Michael Harnett's *The Old Refrain*, the painting with the violin on a wooden door. The inset bookshelves on either side of the hearth still hold a set of *World Book* encyclopedias. The gold-framed picture mirror hangs over the mantle. The end tables and lamps are in their places as they have been since I can remember. This is a familiar place. This is a sacred place. Much of who I am, shaped by interaction with my mother and father, happened here.

My mother was a Sunday-hat wearing, fast-walking whirlwind amalgam of Mary and Martha, with the Martha side just outweighing the Mary side. Today, she gets out of her wheelchair only to walk down a hallway; and instead of a fashionable chapeau, she wears a nondescript hearing aid. Once upon a time in this sacred space, she was a consummate hostess, caregiver, nurturer, and teacher,

giving herself away as most mothers do for their families. For a good bit of my early life, she was the only one to clip my toenails.

Which brings me to the subject of Jesus' feet. Jesus walked from Galilee to Jerusalem and all points in between. And despite the fact that he likely wore some kind of sandal, his feet certainly displayed the marks of his travels. Those were the feet that extended out from the table at the home of Mary and Martha and Lazarus. Those were the vulnerable, road-weary feet that Mary took into her hands to cover with twelve ounces of soothing, aromatic ointment. Those were the feet soon to be spiked to a wooden beam for the salvation of the world. Mary's extravagant hospitality was a sacrament, an offering of herself to God. It was an enormous sacrifice of money and a risk of her standing in the community (letting her hair down and touching a man's feet). And it was a sign, a clear confirmation of the purpose to which Jesus had committed himself. Though she was Jesus' friend, she had done what any good mother would do. And when she finished her anointing, she must have smelled the powerful scent of the nard still in her hair.

Which brings me to the subject of the disciples' feet. They had followed Jesus from Galilee to Jerusalem and all points in between. The disciples' feet had to be as road worn as Jesus' feet. Now here they were, extending around a table in an upper room, no less a sacred space than the home of Mary and Martha. These were the feet Jesus stooped to touch with dripping hands, rough carpenter hands that removed the grime from between the toes and in the lines around the heel. These were the feet that he dried with a towel so that they could slip back into sandals and soon flee from his side in fear and confusion. Jesus' extravagant hospitality was a sacrament of service, a sacrifice that would only fully be revealed later on the cross, and a symbol of the purpose to which he was calling his disciples. He had only done what his Father would do. And when he finished his washing, his robe must have remained damp from the water (John 13:1-15).

Which brings me back to my mother. Once upon a time, she was the sacramental anointer, the sacrificial giver, the one whose purpose it was to witness to the gospel for those in her charge. Now she can no longer perform those roles. She is not able. Those roles are now for someone else to perform. And as I sit in the sacred space that once was her house, I am struck by the meaning of that. The stories of these twin footbaths in John's Gospel speak to me of the profound vulnerability required to be a disciple of Jesus. There can be no stooping that is too low for a disciple of Jesus. There can be no foot so filthy as to be untouchable for a disciple of Jesus. There can be no sacrifice too great for a disciple of Jesus to make. And had it not been for my mother's stooping and touching (among other acts of hospitality) in the sacred place I know as home, I would have not understand fully the stooping and touching of Mary in the home of Lazarus or the stooping and touching of Jesus in the upper room.

Which brings me, well, to you and me. During this Lenten season, we would do well to look for opportunities to make ourselves vulnerable, to make the costly sacrifice, to spill out the nard in an extravagant gesture of gratitude for who Jesus is.

Who needs you to take their feet in your hands and anoint them with the fragrance of God's grace and mercy? Who needs you to take hold of their world-weariness and self-doubt and bathe them in the forgiveness offered by Christ?

1. From *The United Methodist Hymnal* (Copyright © 1989 by The United Methodist Publishing House); 363.
2. From "A Room Called Remember" in *A Room Called Remember*, by Frederick Buechner (Harper & Row, 1984); pages 3–4.
3. From "A Room Called Remember" (Buechner); pages 11–12.

Seeing Christ Crucified

Scriptures for Lent:
The Sixth Sunday
Isaiah 50:4-9a
Philippians 2:5-11
Luke 23:1-49

No surprises in this chapter: Our three Scripture texts all bear witness to the suffering of Jesus on the cross. Even Isaiah's song of the "suffering servant" anticipates Jesus' passion. It is hard to know what more there is to say. Isaiah's lament, Paul's hymn, and Luke's grim narrative taken together call for a deep sigh and a long look out a window. If while you take that long look you don't see anything but the scene outside the window frame, let me recommend some other places to cast your eyes.

First, locate an image of one of Rembrandt's *Head of Christ* portraits (there are several). A single Internet search should populate your computer screen with an array of thumbnail images. Study them for a few minutes. Then choose one of them to make into a full screen image. Take a long look at it.

The American poet Denise Levertov has written a profoundly moving poem entitled "Salvator Mundi: Via Crucis." It is a meditation on the passion of Christ as she sees it depicted in one of Rembrandt's *Head of Christ* paintings. I recommend you locate her poem and read it alongside the Rembrandt you have chosen. It appears in her collection *The Stream & the Sapphire: Selected Poems on Religious Themes* and the anthology *Divine Inspiration: The Life of Jesus in World Poetry*. Levertov observes that what Rembrandt didn't show in his painting is what she calls "Incarnation's heaviest weight," namely the desire "to step back from what He, Who was God, / had promised Himself. . . ."[1]

Once you have completed the readings of Scripture for this week, ask yourself how you would answer the question, What is Incarnation's heaviest weight?

SINGING IN THE DARKNESS
ISAIAH 50:4-9a

Once upon a time there lived a little girl named Meghan. Her home was a cottage at the edge of a dark forest, and she lived there with her brother and sister and her mother and father. Meghan mostly played. She especially loved to sing. Friends and neighbors of the family knew Meghan by her singing.

One afternoon Meghan was playing in the edge of the dark forest when she noticed a path winding into the trees. Not old enough yet to be fearful of unknown paths, little Meghan started out along the path. She walked and skipped and danced a good ways down the path before she noticed it was getting dark. Meghan knew she needed to get back home, but when she turned around to go back, she couldn't see the path. The tall trees of the forest were too thick and what little light was left couldn't get through to show her the way.

Meghan began to be afraid. She took a few steps but finally decided to stay right where she was. She remembered her mother and father saying that if she ever got lost the best thing to do was to stay put. So she did. And as the night came, she began to sing to herself. The frogs and cicadas sang with her until Meghan was no longer afraid. Instead, she was getting sleepy. Her head began to nod, and Meghan crouched down in the caress of a great tree root. As she leaned her head back on the trunk, she felt something. It was a nice warm coat someone must have left hanging on a branch. It was a little large for Meghan, but she put it on anyway and fell fast asleep.

The next morning when Meghan awoke, the sunlight had fit the path again, and she was able to find her way home. Everyone was so glad to see her and thankful she was safe. Her mother wanted to know where she got the coat. When Meghan told her what had happened, her mother decided that the best thing to do would be to take it back where Meghan had found it. Meghan tried to take off the coat, but it wouldn't come off. The buttons had disappeared and the fabric had become as firm as a barrel. The doctor was called, but he couldn't do anything. The neighbors came to see, but they couldn't help either. Meghan's mother and father tried everything, but nothing seemed to be able to get the coat to release its grip on little Meghan. So days turned into weeks and weeks turned into months. Meghan became very tired. She tried to play and sing in spite of the coat, but at times it was just too heavy. And sometimes it hurt, especially at night. Meghan was so sad that she stopped singing. By now Meghan's family and the people of her village were sad too. No one knew what to do.

News of Meghan's plight spread far and wide until one day Meghan received a visitor. A man carrying a staff knocked on her cottage door. He had been hearing the stories of a sad little girl trapped in a mysterious coat, and he had come to see her for himself. After greeting Meghan's mother and father and brother and sister, the man entered Meghan's room where she lay in her bed. He kneeled by her side and touched her arm.

"Meghan," the man said, "where did you get this coat?" Meghan looked up at him and replied, "It was in the dark forest where I was lost."

"I thought so," responded the man. "It belongs to the darkness."

"Can you take it away?" asked Meghan.

"No. But I can make you sing again. Would you like that?"

"Oh yes, I would," said Meghan. "More than anything."

With that the man took little Meghan in his strong arms and carried her out into a clearing near the dark forest. He held her very close for a long time, rocking gently, until Meghan fell fast asleep. Then with a great heave, the man threw Meghan into the air. Up and up she went into the sky, and with a flash of light she was transformed into a beautiful golden songbird, her burdensome coat now soft feathers. She fluttered in the breeze a moment and then swooped down onto the shoulder of the man with the shepherd's staff.

"Now child, you may sing forever," he said. And she did.

That story came to me in a dream one night after I had been visiting a young cancer patient in the hospital. Her name was Meghan. She was the first child I had ever personally known with terminal cancer. Witnessing her suffering and pain and sharing in the suffering and sorrow of those who loved her was wrenching and at times almost unbearable. At times I found myself unable "to sustain the weary with a word" (Isaiah 50:4, NRSV) because we were all so weary, weary of asking questions, weary of railing against the unfairness of such a merciless disease, weary of praying to a God who seemed not to hear, weary of hoping against such hopeless odds.

The servant in Isaiah 50, like the psalmist in Psalm 31, experiences great suffering. He is in no way to blame for the suffering but is afflicted by it nonetheless. Yet in addition to knowing that he is suffering, Isaiah's servant also knows that, in spite of evidence to the contrary, "Look! the LORD God will help me" (verse 9). Similarly, the psalmist in Psalm 31 can lament in one gasp, "I am like a piece of pottery, destroyed" (verse 12); and in another proclaim, "But me? I trust you, LORD" (verse 14). As Christians today, we remain subject to the troubles and tragedies that visit us in this world just as Israel groaned for generations under the harsh abuses of oppression and the grief of dislocation. The suffering servant of Isaiah 50 and the afflicted writer of Psalm 31 offer up an audacious challenge to us: When we serve God and hope in God even in the midst of suffering, we bear bold witness *already* to the redemption that God has promised the world, including us.

I shared the story I dreamed with the family of the little girl with cancer. After she passed away, I learned it became a sustaining word in their weary world. Thanks be to God.

What challenges or inspires you in the story the writer experienced in a dream? What does it mean to you to sing in the darkness? How was God present for you during your own times of darkness?

SINGING CHRIST
PHILIPPIANS 2:5-11

He asked me where I was going. I said I was going to Springfield, Virginia, and then I said to myself that I was going to snooze till the cab got there. The hour was midnight. The ride was smooth. The traffic was light. The air was cool. And I was tired from flying all day.

But after riding along with my eyes closed in the polite silence of the cabdriver's company, I decided that I ought to say something no matter how tired I was.

"Where is your home?" I asked. He said Pakistan.

"How long have you been in this country?" He said he'd been here eight years. His family, wife and several children, remained in Pakistan. He sends them money.

"What do you do?" he asked me.

"I'm a minister," I replied. That's usually enough to put the brakes on any further conversation.

After a moment of silence, the cabdriver looked at me in his rearview mirror and asked carefully, "Would you kindly explain to me the difference in your Christian faith and the Muslim faith?" at midnight? in the back of a cab? You've got to be kidding!

This week's lectionary passage from Philippians 2 is a hymn to Christ. Instead of summarizing the events of Jesus' passion, it sings in praise of Christ's incarnation ("he was in the form of God", verse 6), humiliation ("becoming obedient to the point of death", verse 8), and honor ("God highly honored him", verse 9). Biblical scholars continue to debate the origin and purpose of these few verses. Did Paul compose this hymn text himself, or was it already known and in use by the early church? Why does Paul not include some mention of the Resurrection? What does Paul have in mind by breaking out into song here?

Here's what I think. People remember a good song. If a song's tune can be hummed and its lyrics are meaningful and memorable, sooner or later we'll be singing it in the shower. Paul wants the essential good news of Jesus to get stuck in the Philippians' heads. Why? So their heads (minds) will conform to Christ's, "Let the same mind be in you that was in Christ Jesus" (NRSV) or as the Common English Bible (CEB) translates it, "Adopt the attitude that was in Christ Jesus" (verse 5). Sing the song of Christ until you know it by heart, and sooner or later you'll know Christ by heart. Then what happens? You pass along the song to someone else. Or someone over-hears you singing and asks you about the song.

For quite some time after I took that midnight cab ride, I asked myself why I hesitated when asked to explain my faith in Christ. I'm sure any number of people finding themselves in a similar situation would have frozen or fumbled with some churchy-sounding words. In the story of Philip and the Ethiopian eunuch (Acts 8:26-40), thanks to the Holy Spirit, Philip finds himself on a desert road in the back of a cab (chariot) with a curious foreigner who asks him to explain a passage of Scripture. The story doesn't indicate how long the chariot ride was or exactly what Philip said. All we know is that they rode till they came to an oasis and that Philip told the Ethiopian "the good news about Jesus" (Acts 8:35). The time and the talk must have been sufficient since the Ethiopian requested to be baptized, a confir-mation evidently that he found what he had been seeking.

Most of us would prefer that the Holy Spirit keep us off desert roads and out of backs of cabs where we might have to discuss our faith, interpret a passage of Scripture, or explain the church's beliefs to someone. Why is that? Is it because we really don't want to share the story of Jesus? Is it because we don't know how to go about it? Or is it because we don't think we are prepared enough to carry on a meaningful conversation? For many of us, the answer may be "all of the above." My hunch is, though, that what primarily keeps us from sharing the substance of our faith with people—friend or stranger—is a basic fear of inade-quacy. We are afraid we don't know what we believe enough to explain it. We are afraid we don't know the Bible enough to help anyone find his or her way around in it (includ-ing ourselves!). We feel woefully inadequate to the task of getting into the chariots of contemporary seekers.

That night in the cab, after I rubbed the blur from my eyes and took a deep breath, I remem-bered a song I had been studying in my DISCIPLE Bible study class. The song was Philippians 2:5-11. It hits the high points of the gospel pretty well. So I started there, hop-ing that in the wee hours of the night, I had enough of the mind of Christ to make sense of what that meant. Then I asked my driver about who God was for Mus-lims. We talked the whole way home. Basically, though, I just sang the good news of Jesus as best as I could at half past midnight in the back of a cab to a stranger from a foreign land. I might suggest that during Lent you commit this little Pauline hymn text to memory in case you find yourself in the back of a cab and you're asked to sing.

How do you feel about sharing your Christian faith with a stranger? Have you had an experience similar to the one described above? What was it like for you?

A CENTURION PRAISES GOD
LUKE 23:1-49

On Sunday mornings during Lent, my Bible study class has been following the story of Jesus by comparing how each of the Synoptic Gospels (Matthew, Mark, and Luke) recounts that story. What has amazed us at times is what meanings can be gleaned from exploring some of the slightest differences in their tellings, especially in the Passion narrative. It is clear that all four Gospel writers believed that Jesus' suffering and crucifixion were central to understanding his identity and his purpose. Many Jews and others had been subjected to Roman-style punishment, but Jesus was not just any Jew, not just anybody.

All four Gospels describe Jesus' crucifixion in much the same way; the events are grim, and the horror is shown for what it is. A few details differ from account to account. Only in Matthew are we told that at Jesus' death an earth-

quake shook the ground and caused tombs to split open and the dead to rise (Matthew 27:51-52). Matthew's detail underscores the fact that this crucifixion was no ordinary execution but one that would turn the world upside down. Only Matthew and Mark report Jesus crying out from the cross, "My God, my God, why have you forsaken me?" (Matthew 27:46; Mark 15:34, NRSV). Perhaps Matthew followed Mark's lead in highlighting the pain of abandonment Jesus felt in his suffering, and by inference, the pain God must have shared with his beloved son. Only in John do we learn that Jesus' side was pierced by one of the soldiers, spilling blood and water, a sign perhaps that Jesus' sacrifice was truly an offering, a sacrament of divine love (John 19:34).

Then there is Luke. In this week's Gospel reading, a portion of the Passion narrative, two remarkable details are found only in Luke's version. First, only in Luke do we hear one of the two criminals being crucified with Jesus tell him, "Remember me when you come into your kingdom" (Luke 23:42). In fact, right before he addresses Jesus, the criminal proclaims that Jesus is being unfairly punished for he "has done nothing wrong" (verse 41). How does he know this? Was he once a bystander in a crowd of people when Jesus came by teaching and proclaiming the kingdom of God? Did he witness Jesus drive a demon away? Was he a friend of one of the blind or lame or deaf people that Jesus healed? Had he overheard Jesus tell the parable of the prodigal son? Somehow this criminal hanging on a cross beside Jesus knew something about Jesus that compelled him to bear witness to it. And in so doing, he conveys Luke's message of radical inclusion: No one is ever outside the possibility of God's redeeming mercy. "Jesus, remember me" can be anyone's prayer at any time.

Second, the Roman centurion who stands at the foot of the cross appears in the Passion narratives of Matthew, Mark, and Luke. In all three accounts, the centurion utters a response to seeing Jesus take his last breath. Matthew 27:54 and Mark 15:39 (both NRSV) record his words as, "Truly this man was God's Son!" Luke, however, is the only Gospel writer to record the centurion saying this: "Certainly this man was innocent" (Luke 23:47, NRSV). Innocent? Why innocent? What could that mean? Some Bibles will include a marginal note that suggests an alternative word: *righteous*. The CEB as well as the NIV opt for that word. And while the word *righteous* sounds like it might be a better fit, let's stay with this word *innocent*.

Throughout Luke's Gospel, Jesus seems always to be on the side of those on the outside, the poor, the sick, the lame, the hated, the captive, and those who were excluded because they were considered guilty of something—guilty in the eyes of those who wielded religious and political power like a club. Jesus was innocent. Jesus was innocent of guile, of greed, of spiritual snobbery, of political posturing, of cultural status-seeking. Jesus was innocent of sin and of succumbing to the temptations of pride and power. Jesus was innocent of violence, of vice, and of all things evil in the world. So in that sense, he was falsely condemned and falsely executed. The centurion was exactly right: Jesus was innocent. Luke wants that to be made clear. In fact, recall that the penitent criminal had already defended Jesus' innocence. And Pilate had declared Jesus innocent three times; he even reported that Herod had pronounced Jesus innocent (verses 4, 14, 15, 22). So the centurion's proclamation, when it comes, is not new; others had said the same thing. What is unique about his statement is that it is uttered as an expression of praise; Luke even says that before he spoke out loud, the centurion "praised God" (verse 47).

The centurion praised God. His words sing to us and inspire us to sing praises to God. Why? Jesus died as one who lived and breathed and walked through our world yet remained unsullied by its darkness and sin. In fact, Jesus' innocent death highlights the weight of guilt that humankind bears, a weight that humankind can never take away on its own, a weight that implicates us all in Jesus' death. There's something to contemplate this Lent. Jesus lived like he died, innocent, righteous. We live like we will die, sinful, unrighteous. Paul put it frankly: "Both Jews and Greeks are all under the power of sin. As it is written, 'There is no righteous person, not even one' " (Romans 3:9-10). In spite of the many ways we seek to justify ourselves, to undo our own wrongdoing and self-centeredness, to merit God's love, we will always fail because our efforts have no power. The power to justify us, to forgive us, to love us belongs to God. According to Luke, that power was made mani-fest through the death of an innocent Savior, a death that, once and for all, bridged the huge chasm between humankind's unright-eousness and God's holiness. Praise God.

What about Jesus inspires you to sing praises to God?

1. From "Salvator Mundi: Via Crucis" by Denise Levertov, in *Divine Inspiration: The Life of Jesus in World Poetry*, edited by Robert Atwan, George Dardess, and Peggy Rosenthal (Oxford University Press, 1998).

A New Day

Scriptures for Lent:
Easter Sunday
Acts 10:34-43
1 Corinthians 15:19-26
Luke 24:1-12

It is Easter Sunday. Again. What to wear? How often does this High Holy Day boil down to appearances? Why does it matter what we look like when we arrive at church on Easter Sunday? What difference does it make that all of our family members are present and accounted for and appropriately dressed and coiffed? Well, in one sense, what we show up looking like on Easter Sunday does not matter, at least not to the risen Christ who left his linen wrappings behind in the empty tomb, apparently having no use for such outerwear any longer. In another sense, however, according to our readings for this Sunday, all from the New Testament, the way we show up on Easter does matter.

Peter's acceptance of Cornelius and his household into the new community of Easter people inaugurated a new day for race relations in the early church. Jew and Gentile Christians could show up together for Easter worship no longer concerned about what and what not to eat, that is, what appeared to divide them. Christ has set a new table.

For the Corinthians fumbling with knotty details of their afterlife appearances, Paul's word comes as a sharp blade, cutting to the heart of the Easter story: Christ has died, Christ is risen, Christ will come again. Christ's death has signaled a new day for the entire world. Death is done. And with death out of the way, no one need live the same way ever again.

Luke's account of the resurrection of Jesus describes the very first Easter, the best new day of all. The day those first witnesses stumbled and stuttered into believing that something had taken place that had never taken place before. Their varied responses show would-be believers how to respond every Easter. One word: *dance.*

As you read and reflect on this Sunday's Scriptures, here are some suggestions:

- Take twenty minutes one morning to listen to Aaron Copland's "Appalachian Spring." Next listen to Handel's "Hallelujah" Chorus; it is my favorite piece of music to hear at Easter. It is a glorious orchestral hymn of joy and new life, concluding with the Shaker tune "Simple Gifts."
- Read Gerard Manley Hopkins' poem "Easter Communion."[1]
- Locate some paintings of the risen Jesus appearing to various people such as Henry Ossawa Tanner's *The Three Marys*, Rembrandt's *The Incredulity of St. Thomas*, and Correggio's *Noli Me Tangere*. Pay attention to gestures and postures and consider what kinds of responses to Christ they signify.

NO PARTIALITY
ACTS 10:34-43

Acts 10:34-43 is part of a larger narrative section that actually begins at the close of Acts 9. Acts 9:32—11:18 mark a major turning point in the Book of Acts and in the missional history of the early church. Philip's work had already pushed the church out from Jerusalem. But how much further did "to the end of the earth" really mean (Acts 1:8)?

Before we deal with the lectionary passage, let us follow the story of Peter's meeting with the Roman centurion Cornelius starting in Acts 10. Let's view it through the eye of a camera. First we fade in on the city of Caesarea, a strategic Roman port city on the glittering coast of the Mediterranean. Pan eastward and angle in on the residential areas and zoom into a window where we see a decorated soldier named Cornelius, on his knees for afternoon prayers. Why, he's an apparently a God-fearing Gentile, praying like a devout Jew and giving to the poor in his community! Wow! Suddenly he is startled by an angel's visitation and a strange command to seek out a Jew named "Simon, the one known as Peter" (verse 5). So here we meet an outsider to a community of faith, striving mightily to gain access inside. Fade out.

Fade back into an aerial shot along the road going to Joppa, about thirty miles south, to the home of Simon the tanner, where Peter is lodging. He's hungry and his stomach is growling (maybe from fasting), and he also is on his knees in prayer on a hot rooftop at noon. Not surprising he sees a vision of his own. Only what Peter sees is no angel but an unbelievable array of forbidden meat on a big picnic blanket, and with this vision comes the command to have a seat and dig in. Peter, the devout Jew, is shocked. What? A Jew eat a pig or a lizard? You gotta be kidding. Even after hearing the invitation three times to eat anything on the menu, Peter just scratches his head "bewildered" (verse 17).

Keep in mind that Torah had set forth a host of dietary restrictions for a very good reason, as a means to identify God's people as being holy, set apart, and guided first of all by the claims of a holy God rather than by the whims of an unholy culture. To the Jew, following Torah was a matter of community life or death. No wonder Peter was puzzled.

Then the camera cuts away from Peter stewing on the rooftop. The search party sent by Cornelius suddenly appears at the gate of the tanner's house. Imagine Peter's reaction when he hears the Holy Spirit insist that he answer the door and, of all the outrageous acts, invite three Gentiles into a Jewish home to share a meal and to stay the night. It wasn't even Peter's house. You gotta be kidding.

Cut to commercial, and then it's the next day. The scene now follows Peter who agrees to take a few of his friends (all devout and circumcised Jews, by the way) and travel to the house of this Gentile, Cornelius. When Peter arrives, Cornelius is waiting and falls on his face in sheer reverence. "Come in," he says. "I've invited my family and a few friends to hear you speak." Now Peter is confronted again with the prospect of violating Torah. No observant (clean) Jew could enter a non-Jewish (unclean) household; but after Peter chats with his would-be host (cue dramatic music here), he goes into the house. That is a gospel moment if ever there was one.

The next scene, we might imagine, takes place as people sit about, mingle, or listen in as Peter tries to make sense of the work of the Holy Spirit and Cornelius tells his side of the story. And then the invitation is given to Peter: Here we all are. We are ready to listen to you. The camera turns full on Peter, and I imagine seeing his eyes dart around the room and his jaw muscles clench. This is the moment of conversion, but not for Cornelius and his household quite yet. This is the moment of Peter's conversion. What is he to think? More to the point: What will this Jewish follower of Jesus say to a house full of Gentiles?

"I really am learning that God doesn't show partiality to one group of people over another" (verse 34), admits Peter; and with that statement and the rest of his brief sermon, the church is on its way to the ends of the earth. All ethnic or cultural or geographical barriers that could block a person's access to God's promise of forgiveness and new life were removed. The Holy Spirit falls upon Cornelius and all in earshot of Peter; they don't even get a chance to say, "Hey, we believe!" before they are praising God and speaking in tongues. The Holy Spirit was apparently quite satisfied with their piety and readiness to be filled. What else could Peter do but baptize them all, the whole household, to the absolute astonishment of the "circumcised believers who had come with

Peter" (verse 45). And my guess is their astonishment was as much due to the transformation of Peter as to the inclusiveness of the Holy Spirit. Anyway, after everyone dries off, Cornelius invites Peter to stay a few days longer. And wouldn't you like to know what kind of food this Jew and Gentile shared around the dinner table?

Peter was converted in a vision to the idea that God doesn't show partiality. When distinctiveness as God's people (read: special status) becomes an end in itself, for anyone else it becomes a dead end. Know anyone still needing to be converted?

What feelings or thoughts do you have when you read about Peter's new insight in Acts 10:34 that "God doesn't show partiality to one group of people over another"? What fences do you see that make it hard for today's Corneliuses to gain access to Christ's table?

THE DEATH OF DEATH
1 CORINTHIANS 15:19-26

I read Stanley Hauerwas like I drink strong coffee; my system needs a jolt now and again. Read something he has written whether you agree with it or not. On the meaning of Christ's death and resurrection and the state of American Christianity, Dr. Hauerwas has much to say. I would refer you to his many books and articles in print and posted online at the Australian

Broadcasting Corporation's Religion and Ethics website.[2] I'd advise sitting down when you read him. In one recent article I read, Dr. Hauerwas makes this observation:

> If I am right about the story that shapes the American self-understanding, I think we are in a position to better understand why 11 September 2001 had such a profound effect on the self-proclaimed "most powerful nation in the world." The fear of death is necessary to insure a level of cooperation between people who otherwise share nothing in common. In other words, they share nothing in common other than the presumption that death is to be avoided at all costs. That is why in America hospitals have become our cathedrals and physicians are our priests. . . . America is a culture of death because Americans cannot conceive of how life is possible in the face of death. And thus 'freedom' comes to stand for the attempt to live as though we will not die.[3]

There's a shot of theological espresso for you. You're sitting up straight now, I bet. Take a moment to consider Hauerwas' claim. To what extent is the avoidance of death at all costs the unseen undertow that propels us through our lives? Are there signs that we indeed attempt to live as though we will not die? Does the very reality of death sometimes make us want to cower in fear and dread?

If you read around in the commentaries on Paul's Corinthian correspondence, you will likely pick up that the Corinthian believers Paul was writing to had some peculiar notions about what happens to people after death. Some evidently believed nothing happened. Some were sure something happened but wanted also to be sure what they looked like in the afterlife. Some were convinced a baptismal ritual could work as a kind of proxy vote in favor of someone else's resurrection. Paul essentially tells the Corinthians that they have missed the point. They have jumped so quickly to Jesus' resurrection and begun to speculate on how that benefits them that they have bypassed the equally crucial truth of Jesus' death and how that benefits them.

"Everyone dies in Adam," Paul says (verse 22). Everyone. That is point number one. Jesus' dying on the cross cannot be separated from his resurrection. That double-sided event is what defeats the last enemy, death. The operative word is *defeat,* not take away or soften or sugarcoat or crush up like a bitter pill in applesauce. The crucified and risen Christ destroys death's power to destroy. Sounds crazy, doesn't it? Paul knew that, writing, "We preach Christ crucified, which is a scandal to Jews and foolishness to Gentiles" (1 Corinthians 1:23). The cross continues to defy the wisdom of the world. Be honest: It even embarrasses us sometimes.

The truth is, though, there is no escaping death. Living in ways that deny or avoid or euphemize death and its ultimate destruction of the human body is to misunderstand what Jesus accomplished on the cross, and looking only to Christ as a spiritual escape plan is to misunderstand what he promises in his resurrection.

Here's Hauerwas again:

> The resurrected Christ is the crucified Christ. Only such a Christ, moreover, can save us. For Jesus is the Christ, being for us this particular man making possible a particular way of life that is an alternative to the world's fear of one like Jesus. Christians have no fantasy that we may get out of life alive. Instead we have a saviour who was in every way like us, yet also fully God. Jesus is not 50% God and 50% man. He is 100% God and 100% man—he is the incarnation making possible a way to live that constitutes an alternative to all politics that are little less than conspiracies to deny death.[4]

"Christ has died; Christ is risen; Christ will come again."[5] Many Christians recite those words regularly in worship as part of the liturgy of Holy Communion. Those words are intended to signify that the one who speaks them lives differently because of the truth of the words. Hauerwas' point is that Christ's death changes the way we live, not the way we die. We live knowing full well that we will die, but we also live knowing full well that our death is not the end of our story. Death has forever lost its sting because of the cross.

When I make my rounds through the cancer wing of the hospital, I mostly encounter people hanging onto their lives. They grip the sheets of their bedrails with white knuckles. They and their caregivers keep a close eye on the tubes that bring them their life-saving intravenous drugs. They look and talk afraid. One time I walked into a room and was greeted by a couple that was clearly in the midst of joyous conversation. The wife was the patient, but the husband was sitting in the bed with her, their hands intertwined. Without hesitation they welcomed me into their presence (even though they didn't know me from Adam), and we engaged in almost half an hour of story sharing and laughter. Before I left they prayed for me. And as I walked down the hall, I realized that the subjects of the wife's cancer, pain, suffering, treatments, or prognosis had never came up. Forgot to talk about how she was dying.

Death is that great and terrible mystery that we can never seem to get control over, no matter how hard we try. And we try hard. But according to Paul, thanks to what Jesus has done in his death and resurrection, God has taken full control. The pressure is off. We are made alive in Christ so live till you hear the trumpet sound!

What thoughts or feelings emerge for you when you consider the reality of death? What comes to mind when you reflect on the promise of life in Christ?

LORD OF THE DANCE
LUKE 24:1-49

One of my favorite hymns is "Lord of the Dance" (set to the lovely Shaker tune) in which the whole story of Christ, from Christmas to Easter, is told as if it were a great dance. The dance of God.[6]

Of all the colors of springtime, one of my absolute favorites is the yellow of the forsythia bush. Forsythia always seems to be among the first to challenge the still-grey of winter. And when I see some, the spindly branches are always waving wildly in the wind. The dance of creation. What is Easter like for you? Do you find yourself breathless at the reading of the familiar gospel narrative? Are you astounded anew at the unbelievable claim the church makes that Jesus rose from the dead? Do you squint in the bright Easter sunlight, taking notice of all the new blossoms and blooms swaying in the warm breeze, and making the connection between creation's new birth and Christ's resurrection? Do you ever feel the urge to dance on Easter morning? Sometimes I don't either.

In Luke's account of Easter morning (Chapter 24), the principal characters are women (three of them named—two Marys and a Joanna) and Peter. As I read the story of these first twelve verses, these first witnesses to the empty tomb engage in a kind of liturgical dance of response. The women enter the tomb expecting to prepare a dead body for permanent burial. They carry spices and ointments in their arms. They are most likely mournful, shoulders slumped, mouth drawn down, eyes reddened from crying. When they discover no stone covering the entrance and no Jesus, they straighten up in bewilderment, drop their spice bags, grip each other for support, and huddle together to whisper their theories of what has taken place. While they puzzle over this strange situation, they are knocked to their knees by the out-of-the-blue appearance of two men in white. Luke tells us that the women are terrified. They bow their shocked faces to the ground. Then they are told to think hard, to recall exactly what Jesus told them . . . that he would rise on the third day. Of course! They should have remembered! Up they spring and off they run to tell Jesus' closest disciples and friends (all of whom had also forgotten or dismissed Jesus' words). Down, up, huddled, down, up and off running, the women move in a rhythmic pattern as if choreographed, as if they are dancing. It is not so much a dance of joy but a dance of dawning awareness, a dance that signals the range of emotional response they have to the fantastic truth of Jesus' resurrection.

And let's not forget Peter. He dances too. He started a bit earlier, though, around the courtyard of the high priest. Crouching in a shadow, he is spotted by someone and labeled as a follower of Jesus. He spins away to hide his face and spits out a denial. He moves in the firelight, a body in fearful retreat, contorted in a posture of defense; again the accusation, again the spin and the denial. A third time the accusation comes and this time Peter flings himself up into his accuser's face to utter his vehement denial. A cock crows. His head jerks to one side. Jesus looks at him, causing Peter to remember the prophecy, and he falls in a heap to the ground and weeps. His body convulses and rocks in remorse and self-loathing (Luke 22:54-62). This is the Peter who runs to the tomb when the women report what they have experienced. What? What? He is trembling. The story is unfathomable, but he takes off running, weaving though dusty paths, arms pumping, mouth open to breathe, slinging pebbles with every footfall. At the tomb, he skids to a stop and stoops to enter. His whole body is heaving from the exertion. Like the women, he sees no Jesus. He spins away, this time to hide his . . . joy? Could it be true? Up he springs and off he goes. What does the dance of amazement look like?

Funny. I can tell the story of Easter. I can put on my bright tie. I can show up in the sanctuary with a bright smile. I can look to the entire world like I believe the Resurrection. But I don't do much dancing, bodily or spiritually. How can we as Christians truly live in the resurrection of Jesus without dancing? How can I gather with the church on, of all days, Easter morning and experience the astounding presence of the risen Lord, receive the amazing gift of eternal life, or know the unmerited embrace of divine mercy without dancing?

I think I need dancing lessons. I need to be taught to dance my faith. Particularly during this Easter season, all of us who are the church need to be taught to dance in church. And our first lesson should be to read Luke 24 in order to take our cues from the women and Peter and other would-be disciples wandering about in a daze, running back and forth in disbelief, hiding in fear, jumping up in surprise, shrinking back in doubt, stepping up in confidence, huddling together in despair, falling down in amazement, all in response to Jesus' resurrection. Looks a lot like dancing to me.

Maybe that is the point: movement. Maybe instead of thinking of our faith in terms of a steadily paced spiritual "walk," we should think of it as a spiritual "dance," a dynamic movement infused with the spirit of joy, of renewal . . . as if Easter were every day. That, for us, is the gospel truth, or at least it should be. "Dance, then, wherever you may be," goes the tune.

Funny, it sounds like a command rather than a suggestion. Could it be that the lesson of the Easter story is a call to dance, to respond to the Risen Jesus with our whole being; moving here with joy, there with fear, here with hope, there with bewilderment, here with arms lifted, there with hands covering our faces but moving anyway, in any way. Could it be that what matters is conspicuousness? exuberance? Could it be that a proper response to the amazing grace of Christ's resurrection is to step about in the routine of our living with the grace and lightness of a dancer, and in so doing, to stir up among others the spirit of the living God?

"Dance, then, wherever you may be; I am the Lord of the Dance, said he. And I'll lead you all wherever you may be, and I'll lead you all in the dance, said he." Dance, said he. Like the forsythia in the spring.

What display of exuberance might you do this season to stir up your faith and the faith of another?

1. *http://www.poemhunter.com/poem/easter-comm-union/*.

2. See *http://www.abc.net.au/religion/*.

3. From "Best of 2011: The Death of America's God", *www.abc.net.au/religion/articles/2011/08/08/29 47368.htm*, by Stanley Hauerwas (8 August 2011).

4. From "What's Love Got to Do With It? The Politics of the Cross", *www.abc.net.au/religion/articles/2012/04/05/3471386.htm*, by Stanley Hauerwas (5 April 2012).

5. From *The United Methodist Book of Worship*, (Copyright © 1992 by The United Methodist Publishing House); 38.

6. See *The United Methodist Hymnal*, 261.

LEADER GUIDE

HOW TO LEAD THIS STUDY

Following the Way invites adults to explore and reflect upon the Revised Common Lectionary Bible readings for the season of Lent. This Lenten study is rooted in the texts for Year C of the three-year lectionary cycle of readings. Each week you will explore readings from the Old Testament, the Epistles, and a Gospel. "How to Lead This Study" guides you in setting up and leading the study. You'll discover tips for preparing for each week's session, as well as ideas about how to successfully lead a Bible study, even if you have never led one before. Although the Revised Common Lectionary designates a psalm for each week, they are generally not discussed in the main content. These psalms are, however, listed in this section along with ideas for incorporating them into the session. "How to Lead This Study" offers some historical and theological information about the season of Lent and suggests ways that people now and in different times and places have observed this sacred time.

About Lent

As Lent begins, we believers are called to recognize our mortality. As ashes are imposed on our foreheads in the sign of the cross, we face the reality that we will return to dust and ashes. Lent is observed for forty weekdays, starting on Ash Wednesday. Actually, there are forty-six days from the beginning to the end of the season, but Sundays are always considered the Lord's Day and thus not counted in the days of penitence. During the season of Lent we are called to reflect on our sinfulness and our need to be transformed to more closely conform to the image of Jesus. Some Christians choose to give up something to focus more clearly on Christ. Following the pattern of the early church, many contemporary churches instruct youth and adults who intend to be baptized and/or confirmed during Holy Week. More seasoned Christians may engage in spiritual disciplines during this season that will be incorporated into their lives long after Lent has passed.

The Revised Common Lectionary draws together themes from the Old Testament, Epistles, and Gospels to help us make this Lenten journey. Although the readings vary, the three years share the themes of covenant and newness of life.[1] The Scriptures read during Lent teach us that we can rely on God, who initiated the covenant. In turn, we are called to respond by obeying. We are offered new life in the cross where we experience God's transforming grace. The Scriptures help us to discern who we are and who we can become as we live in Christ.

Ways to Observe Lent

Traditions have surrounded Lent for centuries. Some Christians practice serious fasting during Lent. For example, Ethiopian Orthodox Christians fast from meat and dairy for eight weeks. On Easter Eve they attend a lengthy church service that often lasts until 3 A.M. Then they break their fast and celebrate the risen Christ.

Although many Christians give up certain foods during Lent, a British tradition features eating a special pastry on Good Friday. Hot cross buns are sweet breads flavored with spices and fruits. The top of the bun is iced in the shape of a white cross as a reminder of Christ's suffering. In Bermuda, hot cross buns are traditionally served with a sandwich of cod fish cakes. Bermudians also play marbles and fly kites, particularly home-made ones created from sticks and tissue paper. According to local lore, the kites originated with a teacher who wanted to make a visual impression on his students concerning the ascension of Christ. Good Friday here is a day of celebration, with kite-flying events scheduled in many places across the island.[2]

Some communities band together in an ecumenical crosswalk where Christians solemnly progress from one church to another. Usually someone leads the group by carrying a wooden cross. At each stop along the way, there is a brief liturgy, perhaps including a Scripture reading, prayer, and song. This walk is reminiscent of pilgrimages that were popular in Europe during the Middle Ages.

Lenten dramas are produced in some locales. Perhaps the most famous one is performed once each decade in Oberammergau, Germany. This production, which in 2010 drew over half a million spectators, is mounted by thousands of townspeople. These plays that date back to at least the ninth century depict the sufferings of Jesus from Holy Thursday through his death on Good Friday.[3]

Organize a Lenten Study Group

If your church has a series of short-term studies, this Lenten study can be added to the schedule either during the week or on a Sunday morning. If the congregation normally does not offer short-term studies, talk with the pastor and whichever committee is responsible for adult education about scheduling this seven-week study. As you think about scheduling, remember that typically a mid-week study would explore the Scriptures for the upcoming Sunday, whereas a study held on Sunday would likely delve into the Scriptures for that day. If you want to do a study on a Monday or Tuesday, be aware that the first class will meet just before Ash Wednesday. Check the church calendar to be certain that the time you want to offer the study does not conflict with another event, such as choir rehearsal. Also determine which room(s) might be available. Before making a final decision, check with a few key people who are likely to participate to see how your plan fits with their schedules.

Publicity is important for such a study. Be sure that the time, date, room number, and cost of the study books (unless the church will offer these for free) are included in the write-up. State whether you wish to do preregistration, which is helpful for knowing how many books to order. Set a deadline for registration if you choose this option. Otherwise, state that all are welcome. Publicize this information through a variety of channels including pulpit announcements, bulletin announcements, church newsletter articles, church website, church social media, and community newspapers.

Decide what you will do concerning refreshments. Some light, healthy snacks might work on a Sunday morning. Offer participants the option of bringing a brown bag lunch to a midday session. Consider soup and sandwiches for an early evening meeting. Or, you may choose to have only beverages available and suggest that participants bring their own food.

Decide whether you want to hold a preregistration. Whether you do or not, be sure to order enough copies of *Following the Way* so that each participant has the study book. The church will need to determine how much to charge participants or whether to underwrite the cost and announce that the study is free.

Prepare for the Sessions

Leading a Bible study is a sacred privilege. Before you begin the "nuts and bolts" work, pray for the Holy Spirit to guide you and the participants as you encounter each week's Bible passages. Try reading each Scripture devotionally by asking God to speak to your heart through a word or phrase that grabs your attention. Meditate on whatever you are shown and allow this idea to shape your own spiritual growth.

Read the Scriptures and Bible Background for each week's lesson to understand the context of the Scriptures and their meaning. If time permits, consult other commentaries to expand your knowledge. Once you feel comfortable with the Scriptures, begin to plan the session by following these steps:

1. Read the Session Plan from *Following the Way*.
2. Refer to the Session Plan where you will find suggested activities for each Scripture and activities to open the session and close the session. Decide which of these activities will work best with your group. Be aware that the activities generally include discussion, but some include art, music, movement, or other means of learning in addition to discussion.
3. If you choose activities that refer directly to *Following the Way*, mark the places in your book for easy reference during the session.
4. Gather supplies for the selected activities. You will find the supplies listed at the beginning of each activity.
5. Select the hymn(s) you wish to use. If you will sing the hymn(s), notify your accompanist.

6. Determine how you will use the lectionary psalm or other additional reading.
7. Contact any guest speakers or assistants early in the week if you will use their services.

Think about the comfort of the participants in the learning area. Since they will have study books, Bibles, and possibly notepads, your group may prefer sitting at a table. Check to be sure that heat or air conditioning, light, and ventilation will be adequate for the time of day you plan to meet. (Some churches control heat with a thermostat, allowing it to come on only at certain times unless it has been reset.) Also be aware of those with impaired hearing or sight who may hear or see better in certain seats. Likewise, consider how difficult someone with a mobility issue will find it to get to the learning area and locate suitable seating. If the room is not accessible, see if you can be reassigned to a room that will accommodate a person who has physical challenges. Make sure that a small worship table and large writing surface such as an easel with large sheets of paper and markers, a markerboard with markers, or a blackboard with chalk will be on hand. Have a separate space available and a designated worker to provide childcare.

Helpful Ideas for Leading a Group

Bible studies come in many shapes, sizes, and formats. Some begin with a theme and find biblical support for it. Others begin with the Bible itself and unpack the Scriptures, whether from one book or several. Our study begins with the Bible, specifically the texts of the Revised Common Lectionary. Those Scriptures will deeply inform our study. However, *Following the Way* is not a "verse by verse" study of the readings. Instead, we are studying the texts as a kind of roadmap to guide us in our spiritual journey through the Lenten season. Consequently, some of the suggested activities call participants to struggle with questions of faith in their own lives. Our focus is primarily on transformation so that participants may grow in their relationship with Jesus Christ and become more closely conformed to his image. That's a tall order for a seven-week study! And it may be somewhat challenging for the participants since it may be far easier to discuss historical information about the Bible and consider various interpretations of a passage than it is to wrestle with what the passage says to us, personally and as members of the body of Christ, in contemporary life.

Your role as the leader of this group is to create an environment in which participants will feel safe in raising their questions and expressing their doubts. You can also help the class feel comfortable by making clear that you rely solely on volunteers to answer questions and to read aloud. If adults feel pressed to respond or read, they may be embarrassed and may not return to the group. If questions arise that you can definitely answer, do so. If you do not know the answer but suspect that an answer is available, say you do not know and offer to look it up and report back at the next session. Or, suggest a type of resource that will likely include the answer and challenge the questioner and others to do some research and report back. Some questions cannot be fully answered, at least not in this life. Do not be afraid to point out that people through the ages have wrestled with some questions and yet they remain mysteries. If you can truly say so, respond that you have wrestled with that same question and have found an answer that works for you, or that you are still searching. When you show yourself to be a colearner, the participants will feel more comfortable than if you act as the all-knowing expert. You will feel more at ease about leading the group as well.

Additional Scriptures for Lent

Each week the Revised Common Lectionary includes a psalm. On the Sixth Sunday in Lent, two psalms are listed in the Lectionary: one to accompany the Liturgy of the Palms and the other, the Liturgy of the Passion. Since this study will focus on the Liturgy of the Passion, only that psalm is noted. You will find ideas for incorporating the psalms into the session in each session. Also consider reading the psalm responsively from a hymnal with a Psalter. Or, if your church tradition includes chanting, consider chanting the psalm. Some hymnals include dots over the words to indicate when the note should be changed. Many hymnals also include sung responses, which you may want to use.

First Sunday in Lent: Psalm 91:1-2, 9-16
Second Sunday in Lent: Psalm 27
Third Sunday in Lent: Psalm 63:1-8
Fourth Sunday in Lent: Psalm 32
Fifth Sunday in Lent: Psalm 126
Sixth Sunday in Lent (Palm/Passion Sunday): Psalm 31:9-16 (Liturgy of the Passion)
Easter Sunday: Psalm 118:1-2, 14-24

Hymns for Lent

The Lenten hymns sound a somber note, sometimes in a minor key. During this season the "alleluias" fall silent as we consider our own shortcomings and the suffering of our Lord. To help the participants enter into these hymns, suggest that they read them silently, perhaps focusing on a word or phrase that "speaks" to them. Ask them to characterize the hymn as they read. Does it prompt them to feel awe for what Jesus has done, for example, or to empathize with his suffering? After the participants have read the hymn, sing it or read it aloud. Think of ways to divide into groups for the reading such as men read one verse and women another; people on one side of the room sing the even-numbered verses, and those on the opposite side sing the odd-numbered verses; or everyone joins in on the chorus.

First Sunday in Lent
Old Testament: "What Gift Can We Bring"
Epistle: "He Is Lord"
Gospel: "Lord, Who Throughout These Forty Days"

Second Sunday in Lent
Old Testament: "The God of Abraham Praise"
Epistle: "In the Cross of Christ I Glory"
Gospel: "Lord of the Dance"

Third Sunday in Lent
Old Testament: "Seek the Lord"
Epistle: "Guide Me, O Thou Great Jehovah"
Gospel: "Softly and Tenderly Jesus Is Calling"

Fourth Sunday in Lent
Old Testament: "For the Fruits of This Creation"
Epistle: "This Is a Day of New Beginnings"
Gospel: "Come Back Quickly to the Lord"

Fifth Sunday in Lent
Old Testament: "O Mary, Don't You Weep"
Epistle: "When I Survey the Wondrous Cross"
Gospel: "My Jesus, I Love Thee"

Sixth Sunday in Lent (Palm/Passion Sunday)
Old Testament: "He Never Said a Mumbalin' Word"
Epistle: "At the Name of Jesus"
Gospel: "Were You There"

Easter Sunday
New Testament History: "Come, Ye Faithful, Raise the Strain"
Epistle: "Cristo Vive (Christ Is Risen)"
Gospel: "He Rose"

1. To-Do Lists

BIBLE BACKGROUND

Deuteronomy 26:1-11

The Book of Deuteronomy is the fifth and final book in the section of the Bible known as the Torah. This book, traditionally ascribed to Moses, takes the form of a lengthy speech that Moses gave to the people prior to their entry into the Promised Land. Moses died before the people crossed over, but before his death he summarized God's history with them. He also provided valuable preparation for their sojourn in the land that God had promised to Abraham and his descendants. Much of the book details laws and instructions that would enable the community to live as God's people when they settled into their new home.

Chapter 26 begins with directions for the celebration of the feast of the first fruits. Both the worshiper and the priest have roles to play in this ritual. The worshiper gives the basket of freshly harvested produce to the priest, who in turn places it on the altar (verse 4). The worshiper then recites a very specific summary of God's saving acts from the time of the patriarchs to the community's arrival in the land that God had promised. Singled out are the "starving Aramean" (verse 5b), Jacob who lived in Egypt, the Hebrew people who were oppressed by the Egyptians, and the Lord God who heard their cries for help and brought them to this fertile land. There is no mention of conquest; God has given this land to the people (verses 8-9).

This ritual ends with the worshiper celebrating "all the good things the LORD your God has done for you and your family" (verse 11). Although we may expect the worshiper to comment on the abundant harvest that the Creator has provided, this ceremony spotlights the way God has acted historically on behalf of the Israelites to bring them to this place of promise. When the people bring these offerings, they will be living in the land and enjoying the plentiful food that this "land full of milk and honey" yields (verse 9). They will remember what God has done for them and give thanks.*

Romans 10:8b-13

The overarching theme of Paul's letter to the church at Rome, written from Corinth in about A.D. 57, is that salvation is offered by God's grace and received by believers through faith. With its focus on salvation, this letter has often sparked the renewal of Christian faith and life. In Chapter 10, Paul contrasted "the righteousness that comes from the Law" (verse 5) with "the righteousness that comes from faith" (verse 6). The message of verses 8b-13 is that if we confess that "Jesus is Lord" and if we have faith that God raised Jesus from the dead, then we are saved. As Paul wrote here, salvation comes as we both confess and have faith in our hearts.

Paul used several Old Testament quotations to support his arguments. To emphasize the nearness and availability of God, the apostle quoted

Deuteronomy 30:14 in verse 8. In verse 11 he quoted Isaiah 28:16, which is translated "the one who trusts won't tremble" in the CEB. Paul's final quotation in Romans 10:13 is from Joel 2:32. Here he supported his point that all who call on the name of Jesus will be saved.

Verses 12 and 13 provide information about the nature of God. The phrase "who gives richly to all" in verse 12 literally means "being rich toward all." God not only has great riches but also is also willing to share those riches with others. God's willingness to share enables "all who call on the Lord's name" to experience salvation. "All" are included here because "there is no distinction between Jew and Greek" (verse 12). There is one God, and this God is "the same Lord [who] is Lord of all" (verse 12).*

Luke 4:1-13

The story of Jesus' temptation in the wilderness is a fitting beginning for the Lenten season. Although Matthew, Mark, and Luke all tell such a story, the version in Mark is much shorter, and the versions of Matthew and Luke reverse the second and third temptations. Whereas Matthew 4:1-11 and Mark 1:12-13 both placed the temptation story immediately after Jesus' baptism, Luke inserted the genealogy of Jesus (3:23-38) between the baptism and temptation accounts. Both the baptism story and the genealogy declare that Jesus is the Son of God (3:22, 38). That identity is immediately challenged by the devil in Luke 4:3, 9.

Luke 4:1 announces that Jesus is "full of the Holy Spirit." The Spirit did not protect him from temptation, as we might like to assume, but rather led him into the wilderness. Jesus moved quickly from the waters of the Jordan to the desolation of the wilderness. Like Moses on the mountain without food (Deuteronomy 9:9), the Israelites in the wilderness, and Elijah taking flight to the mountain of God (1 Kings 19:4-8), the number forty plays an important role in the temptation story. Jesus ate nothing for forty days. When he was in a vulnerable, physically weakened position, the devil came to test him. The first temptation, to turn stones into bread, was especially challenging to one who was so hungry.

In response to Satan's temptations, Jesus quoted Scripture, particularly relying on Deuteronomy. He cited Deuteronomy 8:3 to emphasize that bread alone (the meeting of bodily requirements) is not all that is necessary for life (Luke 4:4). Jesus chose to trust God rather than Satan to provide for his needs. In the second temptation, the devil offered Jesus authority over "all the kingdoms of the world" (verse 5). This temptation is ironic because Jesus already had authority from God. He responded in verse 8 with the command from Deuteronomy 6:13 that only God is to be worshiped and served. Using a quotation from Psalm 91:11-12 concerning the protection of angels, Satan tempted Jesus to put God to the test by delivering him from death. Refusing to test God, Jesus responded with Deuteronomy 6:16. Jesus overcame the evil of Satan's temptations through both the power of the Holy Spirit and appropriate uses of Scripture.

SESSION PLAN

To begin this Lenten study.

Read and discuss the introduction

Supplies: Following the Way, nametags, markers

Welcome participants and encourage them to fill out a nametag. Distribute *Following the Way*. Explain that you are embarking on a seven-week study. Encourage weekly attendance, but note that since each lesson is self-contained, if any participants must miss a session, they will return to find a new lesson the following week.

Pray: "Gracious God, as we gather to begin this Lenten journey together open our hearts to receive you, our hands to worship you, and our mouths to proclaim your good news to others."

Invite several volunteers to each read a paragraph or two of the "Introduction" and discuss these questions:

1. How does the writer's description of the experiences he has had with people who are nearing death resonate in your own life? What experiences have you had?
2. Death is a topic that most people prefer to avoid. How, though, is it helpful from a spiritual perspective to consider human mortality as we begin the season of Lent?

To explore how a ritual begun early in Israel's history prompts people to remember and give thanks (Deuteronomy 26:1-11).

A   Delve into the Scripture lesson

Supplies: Bibles, Following the Way

Introduce this material by reading or reviewing highlights of the first paragraph in the Deuteronomy section of the Bible Background at the beginning of this session.

Select one volunteer to read Deuteronomy 26:1-5a and another to read verses 5b-11. Note that the first person is reading the directions for preparation and the second is reading the words that the worshiper is to say when presenting the prescribed offering.

Encourage participants to scan "First Fruits and Remembering" to dig deeper into the meaning of this ritual and then discuss these questions:

1. What do you learn about God's faithfulness from this passage?
2. How does the presentation of an offering help people to recognize God's faithfulness?

3. Verse 10b directs the people to bow down before God. Why might they have offered prayers to God?
4. Verse 11 calls for a community celebration. What reasons did the Israelite community have to celebrate before God?
5. What reasons does your community of faith have to celebrate?

B Celebrate what God has done for each participant

Supplies: Bibles, paper, assorted markers, tape or tacks

Solicit a volunteer to read Deuteronomy 26:1-11.

Read verse 11 again and point out that the ritual described here is a thank-offering.

Set out paper and markers in assorted colors. Invite participants to draw a symbol or write a word or phrase that offers thanks to God for something of importance to each participant. The "something" need not be a tangible object.

Invite participants to talk with a partner or team about the significance of what they have drawn or written. Ask participants to tape or tack their symbols to a wall, a bulletin board, or a sheet of poster paper.

To recognize that there are no distinctions within the household of God (Romans 10:8b-13).

A Examine Paul's teaching to the church at Rome

Supplies: Bibles in several translations

Invite volunteers to read Romans 10:8b-13 from several different Bible translations. If possible, have the Scripture read from the Common English Bible, New Revised Standard Version, New International Version, and at least one other translation. Encourage participants to suggest ways in which these different translations provided a fuller range of meaning for them. Then discuss these questions:
1. The quotation in verse 8 is from Deuteronomy 30:14, which is part of an exhortation by Moses to choose life by obeying the Lord. Deuteronomy 30 predicts the Israelites' return from captivity in Babylon, which will be made possible by a spiritual and moral renewal. How do you experience spiritual renewal as you recognize that "the word is near you"?*
2. What does Paul say is necessary for salvation? (verses 9-10).
3. In verses 12-13, Paul declared that "there is no distinction between Jew and Greek" and that "all who call on the Lord's name will be saved." How do practices within the church, particularly related to the way you welcome people, indicate that your congregation believes Jesus is Lord of all, without respect to nationality, ethnicity, race, gender, age, or any other artificial dividing line?

B Hear and respond to a contemporary example that illustrates the Scripture lesson

Supplies: Bibles, Following the Way

Choose someone to read Romans 10:8b-13.

Retell the first three paragraphs of "No Distinction" in *Following the Way*. Discuss these questions:

1. Do you agree that God makes no distinctions? If so, how do your actions and attitudes reflect your belief as you deal with other people?
2. How does your congregation demonstrate the principle that God makes no distinctions?

Select a volunteer to read or review highlights of the rest of "No Distinction." Encourage participants to meditate on this question: Suppose you had been one of the leaders of this Bible study. What thoughts or insights might you have had as you ate your oatmeal pie? Call on volunteers to share any new ideas they gleaned from this activity or any new commitments they are willing to make so as to be more inclusive of all of God's children.

To discover how Jesus was tempted in the wilderness
and how he overcame those temptations
(Luke 4:1-13).

A Unpack the story of Jesus' temptation

Supplies: Bibles

Provide context for today's reading by reminding participants that Jesus had been baptized (Luke 3:21-22) just before this temptation story takes place. That point may have escaped their attention since Jesus' genealogy is recorded in verses 23-38.

Continue setting the stage by offering highlights of the Bible Background. Select a volunteer to read Luke 4:1-13 and then discuss these questions:

1. What does this story tell you about Jesus?
2. What do you learn about how Jesus fends off temptation?
3. What do you learn about "the devil" from this story?
4. What insights do you gain from this story about how you can avoid succumbing to the snares of temptation?

B Dramatize the Bible story

Supplies: Bibles, Following the Way

Choose volunteers to read the narration, read the temptations, and read the responses of Jesus from Luke 4:1-13. Encourage the readers to be as expressive and animated as possible. Note that the writer of *Following the Way* has written the story as a dramatic dialogue. Choose volunteers to read the final paragraph of "Who Do You Think You Are?", the temptations of Satan (written in italics), and the responses of Jesus and explanations that follow (in regular type).

Challenge participants to suggest ways to make this story come alive by adding music, scenery, and special effects. They will not have any of these props available, but prompt them to describe the kind of music they would select for each temptation, possibly even naming a specific song. Encourage them to describe the scenery, perhaps even moving some of it to a more familiar location, such as the steeple of their own church. Ask them to describe any special effects they would use.

Conclude by asking: If we were able to perform our version of this temptation drama for an audience of people who do not yet acknowledge Christ, what do you think their responses might be?

To conclude the session with worship and commitment.

Make a commitment to turn toward God

Supplies: Following the Way, paper, pencils

Direct participants to review the introduction of "To-Do Lists." Give participants paper and pens or pencils. Have them write the words *pray, listen, read, look,* and *be quiet* on paper. Note that our writer has set before us these actions as ways to turn toward God. Whenever we turn toward God, we turn from temptation. Encourage participants to write at least one specific action they could take to grow closer to God. They may be able to "pray daily for those who suffer," or "set aside twenty minutes each day to mediate silently on God's goodness," or "listen to Mozart's *Requiem* as a means to consider one's mortality." Call on several volunteers to name one or two actions they will commit to take this week.

Affirm this commitment by singing "Lord, Who Throughout These Forty Days."[4]

Pray this 13th century English prayer by Richard of Chichester, part of which was popularized in the song "Day by Day" from the musical *Godspell*: "Thanks be to thee, O Lord Jesus Christ, for all the benefits which thou has given us; for all the pains and insults, which thou hast borne for us. O most merciful Redeemer, friend, and brother, may we know thee more clearly, love thee more dearly, and follow thee more nearly, for thine own sake. Amen."[5] Thank the attendees for their participation today. Encourage them to read Chapter 2 in preparation for next week's session and invite a friend to attend with them.

Offer offering this benediction from 1 Thessalonians 5:28: "The grace of our Lord Jesus Christ be with all of you."

2. This Ain't Easy

BIBLE BACKGROUND

Genesis 15:1-12, 17-18

In Genesis 12:1-3, God called Abram and promised to give him land and descendants, who would bless all the families of the earth. This week's lection from Genesis 15 records a covenant ceremony in which God reiterated the promise of land and heirs. The story of God's making a covenant with Abram is again told in Genesis 17, though here God gives the patriarch a new name, Abraham (verse 5).

Although Chapter 12 includes only words spoken by God, Chapter 15 reports that "the LORD's word came to Abram in a vision" (verse 1; see also verse 4). As the text makes clear, the purpose of God's appearance was to establish a covenant with Abram. "The LORD's word," or as the NRSV puts it, "the word of the LORD," is a phrase commonly found in the prophetic literature but found nowhere else in the Pentateuch (first five books of the Bible).

After reassuring Abram that he need not be afraid, God carried on a conversation with him. Abram raised several questions, and God replied. Since it was common practice in the Near East for a servant to inherit his master's estate if there were no heirs, Abram wanted to know if Eliezer of Damascus was the one through whom God's promises would be fulfilled. God made clear that Abram would have a "biological child" (verse 4) from whom would come descendants as innumerable as the stars (verse 5).

Verse 6 highlights Abram's trust in God, and God's positive response to Abram. In Romans 4:3, 9, 22 and Galatians 3:6, Paul summoned this verse to make the point that salvation is based on one's faith, apart from the works of the law. James 2:23 also cited verse 6, but here the point is that works must accompany faith.

After laying out animals that God had specified, each split in half (verse 10), a deep sleep fell over Abram and "a smoking vessel with a fiery flame passed between the split-open animals" (verse 17) signifying that God had "cut a covenant with Abram" (verse 18). It is God who initiates and makes the unilateral, unconditional covenant with Abram.*

Philippians 3:17–4:1

Earlier in Chapter 3, Paul outlined his pedigree as a "blameless" (verse 6) Pharisee who strictly observed the law, even to the point of persecuting those who followed Christ. Having shared this autobiographical information, the apostle then invited his readers to imitate him. Although this invitation likely sounds arrogant to modern ears, ancient Greek and Roman teachers, parents, and the elderly often taught their students, children, and younger generations by encouraging their charges to use them as models for living. Another way to translate the Greek of verse 17, "become co-imitators with me of Christ," puts a more modest slant on Paul's summons to imitate him.

The "enemies of the cross" referred to in verse 18 are not named. Their lifestyle is described in verse 19, though the exact meaning of Paul's remarks about "their stomach" and "their disgrace" is unclear. Whatever specific meaning Paul intended, it is clear that the minds of these enemies are set on things of this earth, perhaps including the practice of gluttony and sexual immorality. People who live this way will experience destruction, not salvation, at the end of their lives.

Verse 20 creates a stark contrast between these enemies and Paul's readers. The enemies are referred to as "they," but those whose "citizenship is in heaven" are referred to as "we." Instead of focusing on earthly things as the enemies do, "we" are looking for a savior, Jesus Christ. "We" are the ones who share the mind and attitude of Christ (see Philippians 2:5). He will transform our earthly bodies into glorious heavenly bodies through the power of his resurrection.

Paul has laid out two options: People can choose to live as Christ's enemies, or they can choose to claim their heavenly citizenship and live as ones who have the mind of Christ. Paul apparently viewed his readers as sharing his commitment to Christ. So that they not waver and cross over to the enemy camp, he encouraged his readers to "stand firm in the Lord" (4:1).*

Luke 13:31-35

These verses are found in the context of Luke's narrative of Jesus' pilgrimage toward Jerusalem (Luke 9:51–19:27). In Luke 13:31, Pharisees urged Jesus to leave Jerusalem immediately since Herod was intent on killing him. Given Herod's track record as an evil ruler who was willing to kill his own family members who got in his way,[6] the Pharisees may well have been correct about Herod's plot. Scholars disagree as to whether this warning is to be seen positively or negatively. On the negative side, Luke characterized the Pharisees as ones who "rejected God's will for themselves" (7:30). Jesus outright condemned the Pharisees (11:37-52) and warned his disciples to beware of their hypocrisy (12:1). Luke reported that they were plotting against Jesus (11:54). Moreover, given these negative portraits of the Pharisees, some have suggested that they were trying to keep Jesus away from Jerusalem in order to distract him and keep him from fulfilling his divine purpose. On the positive side, some commentators argue that the Pharisees' motives are good, but that they cannot comprehend how Jesus will bring about God's purpose.

Whatever prompted the Pharisees to warn Jesus, he did not turn from Jerusalem where the Pharisees said he would be killed, but ironically headed straight for the city that killed the prophets (verses 33, 34). Jesus asserted that he would continue his ministry "today, tomorrow, and the next day" (verse 33). Herod may have been as crafty and destructive as a fox, but he would not deter Jesus from following God's will and completing the work he was sent to do.

In verse 34, Jesus states that he wanted to protect the people of Jerusalem just as a hen protects her chicks, which counterbalances the threat of the evil "fox" in verse 32. But the people were unwilling. Consequently, their "house" (a reference to the Temple or as a metaphor for Israel itself) is abandoned (verse 35). Looking ahead to his arrival on Palm Sunday and his ultimate return as the Son of Man, Jesus said that the people would not see him until they sang the processional psalm (Psalm 118:26, quoted in verse 35) that pilgrims chanted as they entered Jerusalem. *

SESSION PLAN

To consider challenges that God's people face.

Describe situations in which people have trusted God

Supplies: Following the Way, large sheet of paper, marker

Select a volunteer to read the introduction to Chapter 2, "This Ain't Easy." List on the paper the biblical characters mentioned here. Invite participants to add a phrase or two to each name to describe difficult situations each faced. Continue the list by encouraging participants to add to the list names of other biblical characters and their challenges.

Ask: What similarities, particularly in terms of attitudes and actions, do you see among these people who have trusted God in a variety of challenging situations?

Pray these words from *The Imitation of Christ* by Thomas`a Kempis (1380–1471), translated from the Latin: "You, indeed, are the fountain of all good, the height of life, the depth of all that can be spoken. To trust in You above all things is the strongest comfort of Your servants. My God, the Father of mercies, to You I look, in You I trust. Bless and sanctify my soul with heavenly benediction, so that it may become Your holy dwelling and the seat of Your eternal glory."[7] Amen.

To explore God's covenant with Abram
(Genesis 15:1-12, 17-18).

A Reflect on a biblical covenant

Supplies: Bibles, Following the Way

Introduce today's passage by reading or retelling the Bible Background for Genesis.

Select three volunteers to read the parts of the narrator, Abram, and the Lord. Read again verse 6 and ask: In view of the fact that God's promise of an heir to Abram and Sarai had not yet been fulfilled and seemed to grow more far-fetched with each passing day, why do you think Abram trusted God?

Enlist a volunteer to read the quotation by Old Testament scholar Walter Brueggemann in *Following the Way* in the section "Justification by Trust." Ask: What insights, if any, does Brueggemann's quote offer to you regarding Abram's trust? How does it challenge or inspire you? Had you been Abram, do you honestly believe that you would have continued to trust God to fulfill this covenant promise? Why or why not?

B Write a dialogue with God

Supplies: Bibles, paper, pencils

Read aloud Genesis 15:1-12, 17-18, noting that this passage takes the form of a dialogue between Abram and God.
Discuss these questions:
1. What concerns about this covenant are most important for Abram?
2. How does God address these concerns?

Distribute paper and pencils. Encourage participants to write a dialogue with God in which they set before God one or more concerns that currently challenge them. Tell participants that they will not be asked to share their dialogue, so they may be completely candid. Issues might involve a family matter, a workplace issue, a concern about the church, a personal issue such as health, a grief experience, or anything else that a participant chooses. Note that by bringing our concerns before God, we too may develop a greater trust in God's ability and willingness to meet all of our needs.

Set a time limit. Close this activity by inviting participants to echo these words adapted from verse 6, filling in their own names: (Name) trusted the Lord, and the Lord recognized (name's) high moral character.

To investigate role models of Christian living
(Philippians 3:17–4:1).

A Read and respond to Paul's teachings about role models

Supplies: Bibles, Following the Way

Choose someone to read Philippians 3:17–4:1.
Ask: What is your first impression of Paul's advice to "become imitators of me" (verse 17).
Clarify Paul's meaning by recruiting a volunteer to read the section under Philippians beginning with "Hey, Look at Me!" and ending with "a sinner saved by grace through faith."
Focus on Christian role models by discussing the following questions. Use information from Bible Background for Philippians as you find it helpful to augment the discussion.
1. Paul divided people into two camps. How would you describe each camp?
2. How might role models help us to "stand firm in the Lord" (4:1)?

3. Paul wrote in 3:17, "You can use us as models." Similarly, people are viewing you and other church members as models of Christian living. What positive and negative images are Christians setting before the world at large? What changes do you think need to be made?

B Get to know a Christian role model

Supplies: Bibles, Following the Way, large sheet of paper, marker

Select a volunteer to read Philippians 3:17–4:1.

Direct participants to read silently about Miss Annie Ruth from "Once upon a time" through "illuminated by the light of Christ."

Form several small groups. Encourage each group to discuss the following questions, which you will write on large paper prior to the session.
1. What attributes made Miss Annie Ruth such an excellent role model?
2. Think of at least one person who has been a role model in your own life. What attributes have enabled this person to help you walk more closely with Christ?

Bring the groups together and encourage volunteers to state two or three attributes that occurred repeatedly within their groups. Discuss how these attributes may be reflected in the participants' own lives.

To examine the images of "fox" and "hen" (Luke 13:31-35).

A Interpret Jesus' words to the Pharisees and Jerusalem

Supplies: Bibles, Following the Way

Set the stage by reading or retelling the Bible Background for Luke 13:31-35.

Choose two volunteers, one to read verses 31-33 and one for verses 34-35.

Note that we find images of two animals in this passage: a fox and a hen. Discuss these questions:
1. What words come to mind when you think of a "fox"? How might these words apply to Herod?
2. What words come to mind when you think of a "hen," particularly one who has chicks with her? How might these words apply to Jesus?

Continue this discussion by enlisting a volunteer to read the first two paragraphs under "The Fox and the Hen." Then ask:
1. Where or in what kinds of situations do you see Herod the fox at work in today's world?
2. What might Jesus expect us to say or do in light of such situations?
3. Where or in what kinds of situations do you see Jesus the hen at work in today's world?
4. What might Jesus expect us to do or say in these situations?
5. Are there specific situations where, like the people of Jerusalem, the

words and work of Jesus are being rebuffed today? What can the church do to intervene in these situations?

B **Study an example of someone acting as Jesus the compassionate hen**

Supplies: Bibles, Following the Way

Read Luke 13:31-35. Point out that here we see a contrast between Herod the fox and Jesus the compassionate mother hen.

Ask a volunteer to read the portion of "The Fox and the Hen" that begins with the words "In January of 2007" and ends with "a story of salvation."

Invite three people to roleplay a discussion between Trocmé and someone who understands why he acted as he did in order to imitate Jesus and a second individual who cannot understand why he would take such a risk.

Discuss these questions:

1. Many people, including the Gestapo, apparently knew what Trocmé was doing. Why did his enemies allow him to continue his work? (Consider the role of nonviolence in his approach.)
2. What situations exist in your own community that cry out for the kind of compassionate response that Trocmé made?
3. What might your group or church do to respond as Jesus might to these situations? (If a concrete possibility is suggested, urge the group to plan to address the situations.)

Conclude this activity by challenging participants to be open to responding with Christ-like compassion whenever they identify unjust situations.

To conclude the session with prayer and praise.

Worship the Lord

Supplies: Bibles, hymnals

Read Psalm 27 responsively from the Psalter in your hymnal. If the group does not have access to a Psalter, solicit one volunteer to read verses 1-5, a second volunteer to read verse 6, a third to read 7-10, and a fourth to read 11-13. Encourage all participants to read verse 14 in unison as a sign of their commitment to be strong and trust in God.

Sing "In the Cross of Christ I Glory."[8]

Pray this prayer of John Hunter of Scotland: "Grant, O Lord, that what has been said with our lips we may believe in our hearts, and that what we believe in our hearts we may practice in our lives; through Jesus Christ our Lord. Amen."[9]

Thank attendees for their participation today and suggest that they read Chapter 3 in preparation for next week's session.

Close with this benediction from 1 Corinthians 16:23: "The grace of the Lord Jesus Christ be with you."

3. Self-Exam

BIBLE BACKGROUND

Isaiah 55:1-9

The context for this invitation to come and feast is the Babylonian captivity. The people who first heard Isaiah's message were exiles who had been in exile for several decades, dating back to the first deportation in 597 B.C. when many prominent and skilled Judeans were deported, the same year[10] in which King Jehoiachin surrendered to King Nebuchadnezzar. The invitation in Isaiah 55:1-9 offered hope for a better future.

The passage begins in verse 1 with an invitation to a banquet. Money is unnecessary, though, because God, the host, will provide all that is needed to satisfy those who are hungry and thirsty. Isaiah pointed out that the people had wasted their money on things that were of no value. He urged them in verse 2 to "eat what is good," that is, what God provides.

In verse 3, God spoke about "an everlasting covenant" and linked that to "faithful loyalty to David," whose reign was a golden era for Israel. Recall that in 2 Samuel 7:1-17, God made a covenant with David that his house or "dynasty" (7:11) would last forever. Here in Isaiah, God recalled this covenant. This connection is significant, for nowhere else in Isaiah 40–66 is King David mentioned. Moreover, "the holy one of Israel" (verse 5) promised to glorify the people, presumably just as God had glorified David.

Note the imperatives in this text: *come, buy, eat, listen, listen and come, look, seek*. These active verbs cry out for a response. The theme of repentance and return to God, so prominent in this season of Lent, is sounded in verses 6-7. Those who "return" to God will be met with mercy and forgiveness, not because of who they are but because God is gracious and ready at all times to forgive.

The lection concludes with God speaking again in verses 8-9, clarifying that divine "plans" and "ways" cannot be understood by humanity.*

1 Corinthians 10:1-13

In Chapters 8 and 9, Paul has been discussing the issue of individual freedom within the faith community versus the need for everyone to take responsibility for all members of the body. Specifically, he has been talking about how meat sacrificed to idols is viewed by those with weaker and stronger degrees of faith. Those who are stronger need to waive their rights in order to avoid putting obstacles in the way of those who are not as mature. Particularly in Chapter 9, Paul explained how he had "become all things to all people, so [he] could save some by all possible means" (9:22).

Paul warned the church in Corinth with memories of the Israelites who wandered in the wilderness. They worshiped idols (10:7), engaged in immoral sexual practices (verse 8), tested God (verse 9), and grumbled against God (verse 10). Paul used the disobedience and failures of the wilderness generation as an example to the church members in Corinth (and us) of people who chose to do what they wanted. He drew strong connections between the two groups by referring to the Israelites as "our ancestors" (verse 1). This story of the liberated Hebrew slaves thus becomes the story of the Corinthian church as well.

The people with Moses were falsely confident in their ability to withstand temptation. They were found wanting, and that may happen to Christ's followers as well, who Paul perceived to be living at "the end of time" (verse 11). Paul acknowledged that temptation is a universal phenomenon, one that we cannot overcome on our own. We cannot rely on our own strength, nor is there any need to. "God is faithful" (verse 13), Paul reassured his readers. Moreover, God knows how much temptation each person can handle, and God will provide us with "a way out," an exodus.*

Luke 13:1-9

This week's Gospel lection, as last week's, is part of the travel narrative that follows Jesus from the time he "determined to go to Jerusalem" (9:51) until he arrived at his destination on what we call Palm Sunday. Luke 13:1-9 concludes a continuous teaching of Jesus that began at 12:1. Just prior to this discourse, Jesus had been at the home of a Pharisee (11:37). During this meal, Jesus denounced practices of these Pharisees and legal experts. Verses 53-54 report that, when he left the house, the offended religious leaders became proactive in their efforts to entrap Jesus.

As Chapter 12 begins, "a crowd of thousands upon thousands had gathered." Thus, today's reading is part of a very public teaching. Chapter 13:1-9 may be viewed as two parts: verses 1-5 in which introduced two specific episodes, and verses 6-9 in which Jesus told a parable. Both of these sections are fitting for a Lenten study, since both urge repentance.

In Luke 13:1-5, some in the audience raised the example of the deaths of Galileans that occurred at the hands of Pilate while they were offering sacrifices. Apparently, these questioners believed that sin is the root cause of calamity. Jesus firmly responded "no." Sin did not cause either these violent deaths by the political ruler, or, for that matter, the unexpected collapse of a tower. The victims in either case were not more sinful than anyone else. Jesus drove home the point that all people need to repent and change their hearts (verses 3, 5).

Having commended repentance, Jesus then told the parable of the barren fig tree. Although unproductive trees could not be allowed to take up precious land resources, the gardener in this story appeals to the landowner for mercy for the tree, rather than judgment. The fig tree and vineyard commonly represent Israel in the Old Testament. Jesus was warning Israel to repent and bear fruit, for the time was short. If they did not, like the Galileans and people of Jerusalem (verses 1-5) and like the fig tree (verses 6-9), they could perish.*

SESSION PLAN

To open our hearts and minds to God.

Do an "examen of conscience"

Supplies: Following the Way

Welcome participants and offer this prayer: Gracious God, help us to see ourselves as you see us so that we might repent and be forgiven. In Jesus' name we pray. Amen.

Direct the group's attention to the introduction of "Self-Exam" in *Following the Way*. Suggest that participants silently review this material.

Invite participants to relax as you read aloud the five steps of St. Ignatius' "General Examen of Conscience." Pause after each step so that participants have time to reflect on their own lives. After the fifth step, lead participants in praying the Lord's Prayer in unison.

Debrief this activity by encouraging participants to state how this experience affected them. They may comment on their emotional response (for example, surprise, relief, discomfort). Recommend that they set aside time to do this spiritual exercise each day in the coming week.

To hear and respond to God's dinner invitation
(Isaiah 55:1-9).

A Compare a Bible story to a contemporary example of hospitality

Supplies: Bibles, Following the Way

Recruit a volunteer to read "Divine Hospitality" beginning on with "My family and I" and ending with "all fed in more ways than one." Discuss these questions: Was the Christmas dinner guest list surprising to you? If so, why? Were the behaviors of any of the guests surprising to you? If so, why?

Choose another volunteer to read "Divine Hospitality" beginning with "The words proclaimed in Chapter 55" and ending with "Can this be true?" How might this holiday meal be a "foretaste" of God's heavenly banquet? Where did you see grace present in the holiday meal? Where is grace present in the meal that God will host?

Conclude by asking participants to envision themselves at the Christmas dinner and the heavenly banquet. Suggest that they reflect silently on these questions, which you will read slowly: Do you feel as if you belong at the table? If not, what barriers prevent you from feeling welcomed? In what ways are you welcoming others to the table, even those who you may not have expected or wanted to find there? How does God's hospitality bring people together?

B Explore a prophecy

Supplies: Bibles, Following the Way

Read or review highlights of the Bible Background for Isaiah. Recruit a volunteer to read Isaiah 55:1-9 and then discuss these questions:
1. Had you been one of those who had been exiled in Babylon, what response would you have made to Isaiah's prophecy?
2. Look at the verbs (action words) in this passage. What are people being called to do?
3. How would you describe God as a banquet host?
4. Based on the lavish banquet for the people of God, what response do you think folks will make to God's call in verse 6 to "seek the LORD"?

Wrap up this activity with a moment for silent reflection. Invite participants to hear God's call for repentance and make their own responses.

To learn a lesson from the past
(1 Corinthians 10:1-13).

A Consider a word of warning

Supplies: Bibles, Following the Way, large sheet of paper, marker

Select a volunteer to read 1 Corinthians 1:10-13 and discuss these questions as a group:
1. What did "all" of the people of the wilderness generation do?
2. Why was God unhappy with the wilderness generation?
3. How does Paul use the behaviors of the wilderness generation as a warning to the generation in first century Corinth? (See especially verse 11.)
4. What claim did Paul make about God?

Form teams of three or four and encourage participants to look together at "The Idols of March." Prior to the session write the following questions on a large sheet of paper. Post it now for the groups to see.
1. If you asked several Christians to name current examples of idolatry, what kinds of responses might they give?
2. What motivates people to pursue idols?
3. Our writer suggests that the sin that leads us to idolatry is "distrust of God." Do you agree? Are there other reasons that people may choose to put some sort of idol ahead of God?

Bring teams together and wrap up by asking: What do Paul's teachings about idolatry suggest to you about how Christians are to live in relationship with God today?

B   Make a commitment to turn from idols and trust God

Supplies: Bibles, Following the Way, paper, pencil

Choose a reader for 1 Corinthians 10:1-13.

Enlist another volunteer to read the final two paragraphs of "The Idols of March." Ask: Why do you think people may rely more on themselves than on God?

Distribute paper and pencils. Suggest that participants identify possible idols in their own lives and reasons why they may find them so appealing. Encourage them to list these ideas, which will not be shared.

Invite participants to focus on whatever they believe is the main reason for their own reluctance to rely completely on God. Then, ask them to write a few sentences, addressed to God, offering words of repentance and a statement of what they intend to do to increase their trust in and dependence on God.

Conclude by recommending that participants put these papers in the Bibles and refer to them as they continue the Lenten journey.

To encounter Jesus' teachings on the need for change
(Luke 13:1-9).

A   Read about God's righteousness and grace

Supplies: Bibles, Following the Way

Select a volunteer to read Luke 13:1-5 and discuss these questions:
1. How would you describe the attitude of the persons who spoke to Jesus? (Note that they seemed self-righteous, assuming that they were better and less sinful than those who were killed either by Pilate or by a disaster.)
2. How does Jesus respond to their smugness?
3. How would you describe the kind of change that Jesus said must occur? (This change takes place in one's heart and affects how people choose to live.)

Select a volunteer to read Luke 13:6-9, a parable of a fig tree. Read or review highlights of "Grace and Manure." Ask:
1. What two responses does our writer suggest in response to this parable? (One is to focus on God's righteousness and judgment; the other is to focus on the unmerited mercy and patience of God.) What other responses might you suggest?
2. How is God's grace evident in this parable?
3. How would you summarize Jesus' teachings in Luke 13:1-9?

B Illustrate a fruitful tree

Supplies: Bibles, large sheet of paper, marker, plain paper, pencils

Choose a volunteer to read aloud Luke 13:1-9.

Use information from Bible Background for Luke to help participants interpret the story.

Brainstorm answers with the group to this question: What kind of fruit does Jesus expect to see in the lives of those who follow him? (Galatians 5:22-23 will provide some answers.)

Distribute paper and pencils. Encourage participants to draw a tree with circles hanging on it. Then they are to write the name of a "fruit" from the list in (or next to) each circle they have drawn on their tree. Participants are then to select "fruits" that they believe they have borne and write several words or phrases next to each one to describe an example of that particular fruit. For example, next to "patience" they may write "volunteered to help a third grader who was having trouble reading." Invite, but do not pressure, participants to share responses.

Draw the group together and provide quiet time for participants to pray for guidance in developing a fruit for which they could think of no illustration. For example, some may be unable to control themselves due to a temper that flares quickly.

End this activity by challenging those who find that their "tree" needs to bear more fruit to lean on God's grace and mercy so that they may be more productive on behalf of the Kingdom.

To quench one's thirst at God's table.

Worship the Lord

Supplies: Bibles, hymnals, pitcher, water, basin

Set a basin on a table. Pour water into it, raising the pitcher so that all participants can see the water flowing out. Read Psalm 63:1-8. Point out that the psalmist longs for God as a thirsty person longs for water.

Invite participants to pray silently about their own needs, asking God to fill them with life-giving sustenance. End the silent time by reading this prayer: Open our hearts, O God, so that we may repent of our sins, trust completely in you, and give thanks for your rich grace. In Jesus' name we pray. Amen.

Sing "Guide Me, O Thou Great Jehovah."[11]

Suggest that participants prepare for the next session by reading Chapter 4.

Close by inviting everyone to join you in this familiar benediction from Numbers 6:24-26 (NRSV): "The Lord bless you and keep you; the Lord make his face to shine upon you, and be gracious to you; the Lord lift up his countenance upon you, and give you peace."

4. Homecomings

BIBLE BACKGROUND

Joshua 5:9-12

Joshua 3–4 records that the Israelites had crossed over into the Promised Land under Joshua's leadership. As Chapter 5 begins, they are in a period of transition. God had promised this land to their ancestor Abraham, but battles would have to be fought to defeat the Canaanites who already inhabited this land. Three events occurred to prepare the people for their first encounter at Jericho. First, Joshua 5:2-9 reports on the ceremony of circumcision at Gilgal, a word that sounds like the Hebrew word *galal* meaning "to roll away."[12] Males were required to be circumcised in order to participate in the feast of Passover, but apparently those born during the forty-year sojourn in the wilderness had not been properly circumcised. Passover marked the second stage of preparation. The account of Passover in verses 10-12 is the focal point of today's reading. The third part of the preparation for war found in verses 13-15, though it is not part of today's lection, is the story of Joshua's encounter with a mysterious figure who identified himself as "the commander of the LORD's heavenly force" (5:14).

Recall that instructions for the first Passover were given in Exodus 12, just prior to the Israelites' liberation from Egypt. Numbers 9:1-14 records the keeping of one Passover in the Sinai desert in "the second year after they had left the land of Egypt" (verse 1). Now the people will celebrate this foundational festival for the first time in the Promised Land. Joshua 5:11 notes that the day after they ate the Passover meal, "They ate food produced in the land: unleavened bread and roasted grain." This detail, along with the further explanation in verse 12, is important. The manna that God had provided for forty years "stopped." Just how the Israelites got this bread and grain is unclear, but they were no longer relying on manna. This particular Passover marked the end of the Israelites' diet of manna and their movement into the Promised Land.*

2 Corinthians 5:16-21

Today's reading is part of a larger section from 2 Corinthians 5:11–6:13 that focuses on Paul's ministry of reconciliation. Paul perceived himself to be a minister of reconciliation, an "ambassador" (verse 20), pointing the way for people who had been estranged from God to be restored through the grace of Christ. Such reconciliation was made possible due to the incarnation, death, and resurrection of Jesus. As a result of the Christ-event there is now a new creation. The former way of life of believers has been reoriented because Christ has inwardly transformed them. Although society encourages contemporary people to participate in self-help ventures to improve aspects of their lives, what Paul wrote about is neither a piecemeal effort nor possible for us to do on our own. This total transformation is a work of God through the mediation of Christ.

Paul's comments were not simply an exercise to set forth theological ideas. Paul himself, along with the congregation, had experienced a need for reconciliation. In 2 Corinthians 2:1-4, the apostle referred to a painful visit (verse 1). Verses 5-11 clarify that a man in the Corinthian church apparently caused a rift between Paul and the community during a prior visit. The reason for the confrontation is not specified, but "the majority" (verse 6) must have reacted negatively to this man's behavior, thereby causing conflict in the church. The tension was undoubtedly serious enough that Paul deliberately stayed away from this church in order to avoid further pain for the members and, presumably, for himself. Paul had forgiven the one who had wronged him, and he called upon the church members to do the same.

In 5:16, Paul made the point that those who are in Christ no longer evaluate other people "by human standards." Through Christ, "John Doe" and "Mary Smith" have become totally different persons. Each is a "new creation" in Christ (verse 17). Without holding their sin against them, Christ has reconciled them to God. Those who have been reconciled need to become righteous before God.*

Luke 15:1-3, 11b-32

The themes of repentance and reconciliation come to the forefront during Lent. Perhaps no biblical story embodies these themes better than the parable of the prodigal and his brother. Luke 15 includes three parables—the lost sheep, the lost coin, and the prodigal—that Jesus told in response to the "grumbling" of the Pharisees and legal experts (verse 2). These highly respected Jewish leaders questioned Jesus' table companions: "tax collectors and sinners" (verse 1). "Sinners" included people who violated moral codes and anyone who did not maintain the ritual purity of the Pharisees. In contrast to the Pharisees who kept their distance from such people, Jesus lovingly welcomed them.

Luke 11b-32 includes the themes of restoration and celebration seen in the first two parables in verses 3-10, but this story is far more complex. Different titles have been attached to this parable to highlight the perspective of the younger prodigal son, the angry elder brother, and the compassionate father who loves both of his sons. Jesus' introduction to these characters calls attention to their relationship with their father: "A certain man had two sons" (verse 11). The relationship between the brothers themselves was clearly strained, for when the younger returns home, the elder does not refer to him as his brother but as "this son of yours" (verse 30).

The younger son's request to receive his share of his father's estate was unusual and disrespectful, for he was treating his father as if he were already dead. Lest we judge the prodigal too quickly, the older brother, though outwardly showing respect and obedience, responded to his father's pleas to join the party for his brother with a statement revealing deep-seated anger: "For all these years I have been working like a slave for you" (verse 29, NRSV).

Despite the younger son's depraved lifestyle and the older son's seething resentment, the father loved both of his sons. He was so overjoyed with the younger one's return that he ran to meet him. Before the son can even finish his request to be received back as a servant, the father has graciously forgiven him, treated him as royalty, and ordered a grand celebration. Yet the father does not ignore the elder son. Rather, he does all that he can to restore relationships within the family.*

SESSION PLAN

To think about homecoming hospitality.

Hear stories of hospitality

Supplies: Following the Way

Enlist two volunteers to each read two paragraphs of the introduction to "Homecomings" on pages 31–32.

Invite participants to tell stories of hospitality on the front porch or back deck. Perhaps some will have a preference, as our lesson writer does.

Discuss these questions:

1. What are the hallmarks of hospitality for you?
2. When returning home after an absence, what kind of reception and hospitality do you hope to find? For example, do you expect certain people to be there to greet you? Are you looking forward to some must-have food? Are you anticipating finding things just as you left them however long ago?

Conclude by leading the group in this prayer: Loving God, as we reflect on what it means to be your children, we give thanks for your gracious hospitality and warm welcome home, no matter what we have or have not done. Amen.

To learn about the Israelites' early days in the Promised Land (Joshua 5:9-12).

A   Celebrate a new beginning

Supplies: Bibles, Following the Way

Set the stage by retelling the first two paragraphs of "Dinner on the Grounds" on pages 32–33.

Choose a volunteer to read Joshua 5:9-12 and then discuss these questions:

1. What do you know about how Passover is to be celebrated? (See Exodus 12.)
2. Based on your knowledge of the Passover feast, what challenges do you think these people who had been wandering in the desert faced in properly celebrating this important feast?
3. Passover was eaten in the spring on the fourteenth day of Nisan. On

the fifteenth day, the people ate food grown on the land and the manna stopped (see also Exodus 16:35). Why, after God had provided manna for forty years, do you think this bread was no longer available?

4. How do you view this Passover meal as a celebration?

B Recall a special meal

Supplies: Bibles, Following the Way

Choose a volunteer to read the paragraph on page 33 in the section "Dinner on the Grounds" that begins "I'm going to guess."

Form several small groups and ask each one to recall a special dinner or festival at the church they currently attend or at a former church. Suggest that they consider what made the dinner so memorable. If the event they recall was held on an annual basis (such as a strawberry festival), what was the history of this event, and why did it become such a treasured part of the church's identity?

Call the groups together and invite a volunteer to read Joshua 5:9-12. Then discuss these questions:

1. What made this Passover meal in Gilgal so special? (Be sure to note that Passover had been instituted just before the people left Egypt. Now they were celebrating it for the first time in the Promised Land. Also note that the people were eating "food produced in the land" [verse 12], rather than manna.)

2. Had you been among those celebrating Passover at Gilgal, what would have been your reaction to cessation of manna immediately following the Passover?

3. What does the fact that God stopped sending manna suggest to you about God and God's intentions for the people who were now in the Promised Land?

4. What connections can you draw between the special meal that you recall and this special meal in the Promised Land?

To appreciate that God is on our side
(2 Corinthians 5:16-21).

A Describe key concepts

Supplies: Bibles, Following the Way, large sheet of paper, marker, optional Bible reference books (such as a commentary or dictionary)

Call on a volunteer to read 2 Corinthians 5:16-21.

Encourage participants to identify key words or concepts that appear in these verses and write these on the paper. Three important ones are *new creation, reconciliation, ambassadors.*

Form small groups and assign one word or concept to each group. Direct the group members to talk about how they understand their assigned concept. Suggest that the groups look at the Bible Background for 2 Corinthians on pages 87–88. If you have reference books that may be useful, distribute them to the appropriate groups.

Bring everyone together and ask one person from each group to report its findings.

Conclude by asking: How do these key concepts help you to appreciate that God is on your side?

B   Act as an ambassador for Christ

Supplies: Bibles, Following the Way, paper, pencils

Enlist a volunteer to read 2 Corinthians 5:16-21.

Suggest that participants scan "God Is on Your Side" on pages 34–36 to become aware of ways that those who are new creations in Christ can serve as ambassadors in God's "ministry of reconciliation" (verse 18).

Distribute paper and a pencil to each participant. Direct everyone to write examples of the ways that they already act as Christ's ambassadors to help people become reconciled to God and to one another. Go around the room, inviting each person to read two or three ways of acting as a Kingdom ambassador. After everyone has had a chance to share his or her responses, open the floor to comments and questions. Someone may push the discussion by saying, for example, "Joe, you sound very excited about your volunteer work at the county mediation center, and I'd like to know more about it." End by challenging participants to continue working as Christ's ambassadors.

To encounter the radical fatherhood of God (Luke 15:1-3, 11-32).

A   Analyze family relationships

Supplies: Bibles, Following the Way, large sheet of paper, marker

Invite participants to review "Radical Fatherhood" on pages 36–38.

Read Luke 15:1-3 to clarify whom Jesus was speaking to and why these listeners needed to hear what he had to say. (See the Bible Background for Luke on pages 88–89.)

Ask one volunteer to read Luke 15:11-24 and another to read verses 25-32.

Form three discussion groups. Each group is to consider the story from the perspective of one of the three characters: the father, the younger son, the older son. Post these questions for the groups to discuss:

1. How would you describe the relationship between your assigned character and each of the other two characters?
2. What does your character seem to want or need from his family? Is he able to get what he desires? If so, how?
3. Was this character's behavior what you would have expected of him? Why or why not?

Reunite the groups and encourage each one to report on its character. Conclude by asking: Who is the main character in this story—and why? What lessons does he have to teach us?

B   Dramatize a Scripture story

Supplies: Bibles

Choose five volunteers to read the parts of the storyteller, the father, the younger son, the older son, and the servant. If possible, have the readers stationed at different points in the room so that the players can move toward and away from one another, as the story dictates. Discuss these questions:
1. Which character could you most closely identify with? Why?
2. Which character did you feel least sympathy for? Why?
3. If this story were turned into a video, what kind of music would you expect to hear when the father is prominent? When the younger son is featured? When the older son is spotlighted? Why does each type of music (or particular song) seem so fitting for each character?

Close by suggesting that although we may be able to identify with all three characters, Jesus is challenging the religious leaders (and us) who heard him to follow in the footsteps of the compassionate father. Urge participants to show compassion for people who, in their eyes, do not deserve it.

To experience God in worship.

Worship the Lord

Supplies: Bibles, hymnals, large sheet of paper, marker

Read Psalm 32 by forming four groups. One is to read verses 1-4; a second, verse 5; a third, verses 6-7; and the final group, verses 8-11. Point out that this penitential psalm is broken into these divisions by the word *Selah*, which may indicate that there is a pause or musical interlude at that point.[13]*

Post this prayer for the Fourth Sunday in Lent, which you have written on a large sheet of paper prior to the session. Invite participants to join you in reading this prayer in unison: Loving God, you are always wooing us to come home to you. We ask forgiveness for times we have strayed. We also give thanks that you are always on our side and seeking only the best for us. Help us in turn to seek the best for others by engaging in your ministry of reconciliation. In Jesus' name we pray. Amen.

Sing "This Is a Day of New Beginnings."[14] Thank everyone for participating in today's session. Suggest they prepare for next week by reading Chapter 5. Conclude the session by reading today's benediction from 2 Corinthians 13:13: "The grace of the Lord Jesus Christ, the love of God, and the fellowship of the Holy Spirit be with you all." Pause after the words *Christ, God*, and *all* so that participants may repeat what you have said.

5. Amazing Love

BIBLE BACKGROUND

Isaiah 43:16-21

The setting for this lection, made clear in verse 14, is Babylon where the Israelite captives were taken after Nebuchadnezzar's troops sacked Jerusalem. The prophet Isaiah was likely writing not long before King Cyrus of Persia would conquer the Babylonians and allow the exiles to return home in 539 B.C.[15]

In an introduction by the prophet, verses 16-17 vividly recall the Exodus from Egypt. Isaiah remembered how the Lord was responsible for the action that empowered the people to shake off the bonds of slavery and return home despite the seemingly insurmountable obstacle of a sea blocking their escape route as warriors charged at them from behind. God made a way where there was no way.

Speaking in verses 18-21, God declared, "I'm doing a new thing" (verse 19). This "new thing" would entail the people's release from captivity. Although the exiles were told not to "ponder ancient history" (verse 18), the return home from Babylon will be a new and different version of their Exodus from Egypt, a foundational event in their history. During this new exodus, though, the people will not encounter the many hardships that beset them during their forty-year sojourn in the wilderness. They grumbled about the lack of water in the desert; but even before they set out on their second journey, God promised to "put water in the desert" and "streams in the wilderness" (verse 20). The words of hope in this salvation oracle were spoken to people who had lost everything. Their lives in the present were difficult, but the promise of a new future in which they would return to the land of covenant surely buoyed their spirits.

The exiles, according to verse 20, were people whom God formed; they are God's "chosen ones." These people will "recount" God's praise (verse 21). This verse suggests that the purpose of this praise is to make others aware of God's salvation.[16] Just as Jesus commissioned the disciples in Acts 1:8 to be his witnesses, here God's people were to be witnesses for God.*

Philippians 3:4b-14

In writing to the congregation he had founded in Philippi, Paul wanted to assure them that he remained joyful despite his imprisonment. They are his "partners in God's grace" (Philippians 1:7), and he is deeply grateful for their support. Apparently some "people who do evil things" (3:2) have preached a message different from the one that Paul declared. Verses 2-3 named circumcision as a controversial issue. Those insisting upon circumcision were likely Jewish missionaries or Jewish Christians who considered this requirement of the law to be necessary for Christians.[17]

Paul argued that those who serve Christ are "the circumcision," although their confidence is not based on "rituals performed on the body" (verse 3). Here the apostle provided autobiographical testimony to his strict adherence to the law. His heritage was of great importance to him, but he counted that excellent pedigree as "loss" (verse 7) or "sewer trash" (verse 8) compared to what he had gained by knowing Christ. Paul's discussion concerning giving up something of value in order to gain something of far greater value fits well with the themes of Lent.

As an observant Jew, Paul had pursued righteousness as a state that he could achieve if he followed the law and remained "blameless" (verse 6). Yet, in Christ he experienced a paradigm shift. He no longer perceived righteousness as being "[his] own" (verse 9). Rather, in Christ he realized that "the righteousness that [he has] comes from knowing Christ, the power of his resurrection, and the participation in his sufferings" (verse 10). This righteousness of God is based on faith.

Paul did not claim to have reached his goal of "the resurrection of the dead" (verse 11). He had not yet been made complete, but he was pressing on towards the goal. For him this goal was "the prize of God's upward call in Christ Jesus" (verse 14). The apostle had exchanged the certainty of who he was as a Pharisee and the understanding that he could attain righteousness through the law for the value of knowing Christ and, through faith in him, attained a future with him.*

John 12:1-8

The story of Jesus' anointing is told not only here in John but also in Matthew 26:6-13, Mark 14:3-9, and Luke 7:36-50. Although these stories have similar elements, the details and the placement of the story within each Gospel reflect the purposes of each one. Hence, we will focus here only on John's telling of this important incident.

John placed this story after Jesus raised Lazarus (11:1-44) and before Jesus' entry into Jerusalem on Palm Sunday (12:12-19). These events were significant because the raising of Lazarus prompted the Jewish leadership to plot against Jesus (11:45-57) and the entry triggered Jesus' teachings about his death, for his "time has come" (12:23).

Mary anointed Jesus' feet during a dinner at Lazarus's home in Bethany just six days before the beginning of Passover. She showed extravagant love for Jesus by anointing him with "three-quarters of a pound" (verse 3) of spikenard, an expensive perfume that would have cost nearly a year's wages for an average worker (verse 5). Mary then "wiped" his feet with her hair (verse 3). The Greek word translated here as "wiped" is significant, for it points toward Jesus' act of washing of the disciples' feet later in the week and then "wipe[d]" them dry (John 13:5, NRSV).

Judas, who "carried the money bag" for Jesus and the disciples (verse 6), harshly criticized Mary for what he deemed as wastefulness. Jesus immediately squelched his protest, urging Judas to "leave her alone" (verse 7). Jesus said that the perfume was to be used to prepare him for burial (verse 7).

Mary had used it at this dinner as a sign of devotion, but Jesus interpreted her gesture for Judas and others who were present as a sign of his imminent death. Judas, who had been part of the inner circle of disciples, was portrayed as a thief who acted in his own greedy best interests. In contrast, Mary realized that Jesus' time was limited and did what she could to act as a faithful disciple.*

SESSION PLAN

To reflect on God's amazing love.

Recall a story of God's love

Supplies: Bibles, Following the Way

Invite participants to talk with a partner or small group about a Bible story that reflects God's love. They may cite chapters and verses, but a summary or even the title of a well-known story (such as the parable of the good Samaritan) would be sufficient. Encourage participants to explain briefly why the selected stories are so meaningful to them. Perhaps they will recount a Bible story of healing and describe how they also were healed of a disease. They may have survived a major storm and identify with the story of Jesus calming the wind and waves.

Introduce today's Scriptures, all of which demonstrate God's amazing love, by enlisting a volunteer to read the first paragraph of the introduction to "Amazing Love" in *Following the Way*.

To recognize God's love in the midst of God's deeds (Isaiah 43:16-21).

A Hear a promise of a new future

Supplies: Bibles, Following the Way

Recruit a volunteer to read Isaiah 43:16-21 and discuss the following questions. Use information from the Bible Background for Isaiah to add to the discussion.
1. Look back to verses 14-15. What do you know about the God who speaks to the captives in Babylon?
2. What has the Lord done for the Israelites according to verses 16-17? (Be sure participants understand that these words refer to the Exodus from Egypt.)
3. What "new thing" (verse 19) does God promise to do?
4. How will the journey home from Babylon be different from the journey out of Egypt? (See verses 19-20.)

5. Based on verse 21, what does God expect these "chosen ones" to do?
6. How does this passage show God's love in the midst of God's deeds? (You may wish to read the paragraph in "A Brand New Thing" beginning with "Every time" and ending "Old Testament prophet.")

B Envision a new future

Supplies: Bibles, Following the Way, large sheet of paper, marker

Choose a volunteer to read Isaiah 43:16-21, which is addressed to the Israelites who are held captive in Babylon. Ask:
1. What do you think these exiles want from God?
2. What has God done and what will God do for these captives? (Suggest that participants read in unison the list of phrases from Isaiah 43 written in "A Brand New Thing" in *Following the Way*, where God speaks in the first person.)

Begin to think about what new things your congregation needs from God. Make a list on a large sheet of paper. After participants have given some initial answers you may want to prompt consideration of such things as growth in discipleship among the members, new ministries for current members and the community, increased attendance, and maintenance or changes in the building to better serve the congregation and community. Ask: If we could only do one of these listed items, which one would it be? How would accomplishing this change lead us into a better future? See if any participants would like to promote this idea among the church leadership. Perhaps they could create an informal plan of action stating what the group would like to see happen, intended outcomes, and how this change might be made.

*To consider one's willingness to lose what has been valuable
in order to gain Christ
(Philippians 3:4b-14).*

A Interpret Philippians 3:4b-14

Supplies: Bibles

Invite a volunteer to read Philippians 3:4b-14. Form several small groups and read aloud this scenario: A group of older teens or young adults has been studying Philippians. Chapter 3 has raised a lot of questions about the level of commitment Christ calls them to make. Some believe that their walk with Christ is an "add on" to their current lifestyle. Others believe that a radical change is called for, but they don't know what is expected or how to make that change. You have been called in to explain Paul's teachings in Philippians 3:4b-14. How would you explain this teaching in your own words?

Bring the groups together and invite them to tell their ideas.

B   Relate two contemporary examples to the Scripture lesson

Supplies: Bibles, Following the Way

Choose someone to read the paragraphs from "Gains and Losses" beginning with "For many years" and ending with "became distractions for him." Select another volunteer to read from this section beginning with "A couple of years ago" and ending with "losing things?" Discuss these questions:
1. Have you ever had to make such a life-changing choice? If so, what criteria guided your decision?
2. Our study book writer, Mark, also experienced losses and had no control over the circumstances under which they occurred. If you have ever experienced such unplanned changes, how did you respond to them?

Call upon a reader for Philippians 3:4b-14 and then discuss these questions:
1. What do you imagine Paul lost by choosing to serve Christ? (See verses 4b-6.)
2. What might Paul have said to Jeff about the choices he made?
3. What might Paul have said to Mark about the losses he sustained? What advice might Paul have had for Mark about turning these losses into gains?

To encounter a story of love
(John 12:1-8).

A   Interpret a Bible story from different points of view

Supplies: Bibles, Following the Way

Prepare to engage the story by reading the first two paragraphs of the Bible Background for John. Call on a volunteer to read John 12:1-8.

Encourage participants to see Mary's action from different perspectives by discussing these questions:
1. Suppose you were Mary. What prompted you to perform such a gracious, costly act?
2. Suppose you were Judas. Why were you so critical of Mary's action?
3. Suppose you were Lazarus, who Jesus had so recently raised from the dead. What would you have thought about Jesus saying that the perfume had been used in preparation for his own burial? What questions would you have asked Jesus?

Review highlights of "On the Subject of Feet." Ask: Think of someone who is nearing death, either by virtue of age or illness. How might Mary's story of self-giving love affect your own perspective and treatment of that person this week?

B Pantomime and discuss a Bible story

Supplies: Bibles, extra chairs

Select several volunteers who are willing to pantomime the actions of Martha, Lazarus, Mary, Jesus, and Judas. Invite everyone to read John 12:1-8 silently. Those who have agreed to pantomime this story will want to consider actions they may use. When you are ready, have the actors go to a space where everyone can see them. Have chairs available in that space for them. Set an extra chair for the character portraying Jesus to put his foot on, so that all may see. Privately suggest to the woman playing Mary that she move her head from side to side to mimic wiping Jesus' feet with her hair. Cue a volunteer to read John 12:1-8 aloud slowly so that the actors have time to respond with motions. Discuss these questions:

1. Had you been present when Mary anointed Jesus' feet with expensive perfume and then wiped them dry, what would you have said to Mary?
2. How did Judas interpret Mary's action?
3. How did Jesus interpret Mary's action?
4. What might Lazarus have been thinking about his sister's action?
5. What might Martha say to her sister after Jesus and the other guests left their home?
6. Poor people were often the focus of Jesus' ministry. How would you explain his comment in verse 8 to someone who said that Christians don't need to concern themselves with the poor?

To make a commitment to act with love.

Worship the Lord

Supplies: Bibles, hymnals

Read Psalm 126 as a chorus. Choose one volunteer for verse 1, another for verse 2, and a third for verse 3. Invite everyone to respond by reading verses 4-6. So that all participants are using the same translation, distribute hymnals and read from the Psalter.

Provide a few moments of silence for participants to consider how God's love has changed their lives and one response they can make this week to share that love with others. Conclude the quiet time by reading this prayer: O God who makes all things new, we bow before you this day in awe of your amazing love for us. May the thoughts of our minds, the words of our mouths, and the actions of our hands express our love for you as we lovingly serve others in the name of Jesus. Amen.

Sing "My Jesus, I Love Thee."[18] Suggest that participants read Chapter 6 in preparation for next week's session. Be sure to thank them for attending today. Close with this benediction from Philippians 4:23: "The grace of the Lord Jesus Christ be with your spirits." Read this once yourself. Then ask participants repeat these words to one person who is near them.

6. Seeing Christ Crucified

BIBLE BACKGROUND

Isaiah 50:4-9a

On this Palm/Passion Sunday we are focusing on lections that concern Jesus' passion. Isaiah 50:4-9a is the third of the prophet's four "Songs of the Suffering Servant." All four of these songs, Isaiah 42:1-4; 49:1-6; 50:4-9a; 52:13–53:12, are also read during Holy Week on Monday, Tuesday, Wednesday, and Good Friday, respectively.[19] Early in the church's history, Christians interpreted Jesus' life and death through the lens of these songs in particular and the entire Book of Isaiah in general. Isaiah is sometimes called "the fifth Gospel"[20] because of all the important ideas and connections that Christians have drawn from this book to shape their own understandings of who Christ was.

Today's text was written shortly before the end of the Babylonian Exile.[21] The suffering servant that Isaiah described would have resonated with the hardships that the "weary" (verse 4) ones endured during captivity. The servant had been attacked physically and verbally. He suffered insults and bodily harm to his back, cheeks, beard, and face (verses 5-6). Instead of rebelling, the servant was willing to suffer. His obedient suffering links him, in the minds of many Christians, to Jesus. Even in the midst of his suffering, the servant found hope and comfort in the Lord, who would help him (verse 7). The servant was so certain that God was with him that he challenged his attackers to "bring judgment" against him (verse 8). With the Lord on his side, the servant knew that his adversaries could not condemn him (verse 9).

The emphasis in the wording of this third song points toward an individual who is both a teacher and a prophet. God "opened" the servant's ear (verse 5) to receive God's word. This word came to the servant–prophet each day. Moreover, God gave the servant "the tongue of a teacher" (verse 4, NRSV) so that God's word could be communicated. God prepared him to speak to a very specific audience: "the weary" exiles (verse 4). The daily word from God surely provided inspiration and hope to those who saw no future for themselves.

Philippians 2:5-11

This poetic text presents a summary of Christ's incarnation, crucifixion, and exaltation by God. Since Christ's divinity and humanity are both evident in this passage, readers have often turned to Philippians to discern information about his nature. However, this brief description cannot answer questions such as, Did Christ add human nature to his divine nature at the incarnation or, When Christ assumed human form, did he empty himself of his divine nature?

Commentators disagree as to whether Paul wrote these verses or inserted a known text, which may have been a hymn, into his letter. Whatever the source, Paul was not using these verses for worship but rather for exhortation. He urged his readers to "adopt the attitude that was in Christ Jesus" (verse 5) and then explained that attitude. Believers are called to embrace Christ's model of humble obedience.

The hymn itself is divided into two sections, verses 6-8 and 9-11. In the first section, we read about Christ's actions. He did not exploit equality with God. He "emptied himself." He took "the form of a slave." He "humbled himself." He became "obedient to the point of death." He made a conscious decision to take these actions, which were based on his relationship with God. In the second section, we see how God responded to Christ's actions: "God highly honored him and gave him a name above all names" (verse 9). Christ took decisive action based on humble obedience, and God responded to these actions by exalting Jesus. Obedience that resulted in mortal death was transformed into an exalted life. Although Christ received a matchless reward for his obedience, there is no indication in the text that he made his choices in order to gain a reward. His actions grew out of a mindset that focused on his relationship with God. It is this mindset that Paul called his readers to adopt.*

Luke 23:1-49

Just prior to Luke 23, Jesus instituted the Last Supper at a Passover meal, prayed in Gethsemane, been arrested, been denied three times by Peter, been mocked and beaten, and appeared before the Jewish council. Questioned by the council as to his identity as the Son of God, he replied, "You say that I am" (22:70). These words were testimony enough for the council to whisk Jesus away to Pilate for questioning.

The council members made three accusations against Jesus in Luke 23:2. The initial charge is broad; the second two substantiate the first. First, they accuse him of misleading the Jewish people. Jesus' miracles and a message that did not comport well with the teachings of the religious leaders were the basis for the first charge. Second, he opposed paying taxes to the government. This charge would have been more serious in Pilate's eyes since anything that stirred up the people threatened the Roman peace, which Pilate had been set in place to maintain. Third, the Jewish leadership charged Jesus with claiming that he was the Messiah, a king. Pilate asked Jesus if he were the king of the Jews, but Jesus only answered, "That's what you say" (verse 3). Pilate dismissed all the charges and told the leaders, "I find no legal basis for action against this man" (verse 4).

The leaders "objected strenuously" (verse 5) to Pilate's decision. He then determined that Jesus' Galilean residence put him under Herod's jurisdiction. The account of Jesus' appearance before Herod is found only in Luke. Herod was staying in Jerusalem for the Passover and was "very glad to see Jesus" (verse 8). Actually, Herod wanted to see Jesus perform some sign but that did not happen. Instead, Jesus stood mute before Herod, refusing to answer his questions. Herod returned Jesus to Pilate.

The ball was again in Pilate's court, but he still found no legal reason for the charges brought against him. He noted that Herod also found no basis for a capital crime. The crowd, however, would not allow Pilate to release

Jesus but insisted on his crucifixion. By now Pilate had declared Jesus inno-cent three times, but he caved in to pressure from the crowd. The familiar story continues with Jesus' crucifixion and death. Immediately after Jesus "breathed for the last time" (verse 46), a Roman soldier "praised God" (verse 47) and declared the righteousness of Jesus.*

SESSION PLAN

To imagine "Incarnation's heaviest weight."

Reflect on art and poetry

Supplies: Following the Way, copy of Denise Levertov's poem "Salvator Mundi: Via Crucis" (available online[22] and in books)

Choose a volunteer to read the introduction to "Seeing Christ Crucified" in *Following the Way*.

Invite comments from those who, as suggested in the introduction, did locate one or more of the seven[23] surviving paintings from Rembrandt's *Head of Christ* series. What did they see in these pictures? How did the pic-tures affect them?

Read Denise Levertov's poem expressively and then provide a few moments of quiet time for participants to reflect on the following question: What do you perceive to be "Incarnation's heaviest weight"?

Break the silence by offering this prayer: Cross-bearing God, we cannot begin to imagine the suffering you endured for our sakes. Your unfath-omable love for us kept you inching forward beneath the weight of the tree to Golgotha. In awe and humility we give you our praise, thanksgiving, obe-dience, and love. Amen.

To encounter the suffering servant
(Isaiah 50:4-9a).

A   Hear the words of God's faithful servant

Supplies: Bibles, Following the Way

Introduce today's Old Testament text by reading the first paragraph from the Bible Background for Isaiah. Tell participants that the passage we are studying today is the third of four "Songs of the Suffering Servant" (Isa-iah 42:1-4; 49:1-6; 50:9-4a; 52:13–53:12). Suggest that they read the other three songs during this Passion Week.

Choose a volunteer to read Isaiah 50:4-9a. Discuss these questions, using additional information from the Bible Background to fill in gaps:

1. What purpose does God have for this servant?

2. How do people respond to the servant?
3. How does the servant respond to those who oppose him?
4. What evidence do you see here that the servant has unshakeable confidence in God?
5. How might Israelites who were captives in Babylon have responded this text?
6. Following the interpretations of the earliest Christians, the church has continued to see Jesus Christ in this passage. Do you? If so, what do you learn about him from this servant song?

B Relate the servant's suffering to the suffering of others

Supplies: Bibles, Following the Way

Enlist a volunteer to read a portion of "Singing in the Darkness" beginning with "Once upon a time" and ending with "hopeless odds."
Form several small groups and invite them to discuss these questions:
1. How does Meghan's story relate to suffering that you or a loved one has experienced?
2. In what ways does the death of a loved one or other significant loss cause you to be weary?
3. Following a death or other significant loss, were you able to sing again? If so, what motivated you and gave you strength to do so?
Select a volunteer to read Isaiah 50:4-9a. Encourage participants to talk about how Meghan's suffering might have been similar to and different from the suffering of the servant. Think about ways that she may have served as a prophet and teacher for others.
Conclude by emphasizing that in God's own way and time God will help those who suffer. We may grow weary, but God does not. Nor will God abandon us.

To explore a song about Christ
(Philippians 2:5-11).

A Analyze Philippians 2:5-11

Supplies: Bibles, large sheet of paper, marker

Call on one volunteer to read Philippians 2:5-8 and another to read verses 9-11 and then discuss these questions:
1. What words or phrases in verses 6-8 describe Jesus' attitude that Paul called us to adopt?
2. How might things be different for your own congregation if everyone adopted Jesus' attitude? What changes might you notice in worship, education, and committee meetings? (Point participants to verses 1-3 to add ideas.)

3. What happened because Jesus obeyed God the Father?
4. Where do you currently see evidence of people confessing that Jesus is Lord? How do these confessions make a difference in the way people live and how they treat others?

Draw the letter *V* on the paper and invite participants to comment on how this letter shows the movement of this song. Suggest that the letter *V* is helpful in remembering that Jesus was "in the form of God," then emptied himself by taking on human flesh, and humbled himself further by being a slave. Jesus ultimately died on a cross, which is represented by the lowest portion of the *V*. He then was exalted as all people confessed him to be Lord. This exaltation is seen in the rising right side of the *V*. Be sure participants notice that in the first half of the song Jesus was the actor. He made and implemented the decisions. In the second half, God is the one in charge. As a result of God's actions, all people confessed that Jesus is Lord.

B Memorize a song about Christ

Supplies: Bibles, Following the Way

Read Philippians 2:5-11 responsively if your hymnal includes this text. If you have access to *The United Methodist Hymnal*, see page 167. Otherwise, select a volunteer to read Philippians 2:5-11.

Recruit a volunteer to read the paragraphs from "Singing Christ" beginning with the words "This week's lectionary passage" and ending with the words "asked to sing."

Form groups of three or four. Make sure that everyone in the group has the same translation of the Bible. One person will read verse 5, pausing at each comma or period so that the others in the group may repeat the words. Another person will lead verse 6 and so on until all verses from 5 through 11 all have been heard and repeated at least once, more if time permits. Invite anyone who feels brave enough to recite what they have been able to memorize. Ask: What words or phrases stand out for you in the Scripture? What thoughts or feelings do they evoke for you? What do they say to you about God? about Jesus? about human beings?

To review the Passion Narrative
(Luke 23:1-49).

A Tell the Passion story

Supplies: Bibles, large sheet of paper, marker

Form six groups and assign each group one of the following portions of Scripture: Luke 23:1-5, verses 6-12, verses 13-25, verses 26-31, verses 32-43, and verses 44-49.

Post the assigned Scriptures and these questions for each group to discuss:

1. What do you learn about Jesus' opposition or other persons around him?
2. How does Jesus handle the situation described in your assigned verses?
3. What does this passage suggest about the relationship between Jesus and humanity?
4. What does this passage suggest about the relationship between Jesus and God?
5. Had you witnessed the event described in your assigned passage, what would you have said about who Jesus was?

Bring the groups together and invite them to share highlights of their discussion with the entire group.

B Explore three biblical accounts

Supplies: Bibles, Following the Way, large sheet of paper, marker, paper, pencils

Be prepared to retell Luke 23:1-43. Use information from the Bible Background for Luke to help tell the story.

Provide a few moments for participants to review silently "A Centurion Praises God." Enlist a volunteer to read Luke 23:44-49, which tells the dramatic story of Jesus' death. Suggest that participants carefully note the details here.

Point out that Matthew and Mark also include responses by the centurion. Form two groups and ask one to review Matthew 27:45-56 and the other group to look at Mark 15:33-41. Both groups are also to look at Luke 23:44-49. Then the groups are to discern the similarities and differences between Luke's account and their assigned account. Have them discuss the following questions: What do the biblical accounts say to you about Jesus? about God? about human beings? Bring the groups back together to share highlights of their discussion.

To praise God

Worship the Lord

Supplies: Bibles, hymnals, picture of Christ on the cross or a picture of a contemporary person (or group of people) who is clearly suffering

Post or hold up the picture of one who is suffering. Since today's psalm is a prayer and praise for deliverance from enemies, a picture of Jesus or someone affected by the ravages of war would be especially appropriate. Read Psalm 31:9-16 expressively as participants focus on the picture and imagine the individual(s) depicted saying these words.

Encourage the group to pray silently for those who are suffering. Break the silence by offering this prayer: Blessed God, we stand amazed at your

Son's willingness to suffer for us so that we might be reconciled to you. Help us, in turn, to care for those who are suffering all around us. We sing your praises in Jesus' name. Amen.

Sing "Were You There."[24]

Thank everyone for coming today. Suggest that they read Chapter 7 in preparation for the final session.

Close with this benediction from Ephesians 6:23-24: "May there be peace with the brothers and sisters as well as love with the faith that comes from God the Father and the Lord Jesus Christ. May grace be with all those who love our Lord Jesus Christ forever."

7. A New Day
BIBLE BACKGROUND

Acts 10:34-43

In the last of Peter's sermons recorded in Acts, the apostle summarized the gospel message for a Gentile and his household. Before investigating Peter's eyewitness account about Jesus in verses 34-43, we need to consider the context. God had given a vision to Cornelius, a Roman army officer who also worshiped God. In that vision an angel came to Cornelius and told him to send for Peter. Simultaneously, Peter saw a vision of unclean animals that he was told to eat. As an orthodox Jew, this idea was abhorrent to Peter, so he did not immediately understand the vision. In the meantime, Cornelius' messengers arrived from Caesarea and Peter returned with them. As he began to speak to the household members gathered at Cornelius' home, the meaning of his vision became clear. Peter interpreted it to mean that God's gift of salvation was available to all people who worship God and do what is right (verse 35).

After sharing that insight, Peter reviewed Christ's message and how it had spread. The apostle recalled Jesus' baptism and anointing with the Holy Spirit, thus enabling him to do good works and heal people. This information was not new to Peter's audience for he said, "You know what happened" (verse 37) and "You know about Jesus" (verse 38). Peter emphasized that he was not just giving a secondhand report but rather was a "witness" (verses 39, 41) to Jesus' activity, death, and resurrection. He and other apostles even "ate and drank with him after God raised him from the dead" (verse 41). Peter's credentials were impeccable, but there was more. He and the other apostles were not speaking on their own but had been chosen by God and given a mandate to preach to the people about Jesus, the "judge of the living and the dead" (verse 42). Peter proclaimed that those who believed in Jesus would receive "forgiveness of sins through his name" (verse 43). The verses that follow today's lection indicate that Cornelius and his household were moved by Peter's message, for they received the gift of the Holy Spirit and were baptized.*

1 Corinthians 15:19-26

In 1 Corinthians 15, Paul discussed the resurrection of Christ (verses 1-11) and then more generally wrote about the resurrection of the dead (verses 12-34). He finished this important chapter by addressing questions concerning how the dead are raised and the kind of body they will have (verses 35-58). Today's lection focuses on a broader discussion of the resurrection of the dead. Apparently this teaching was necessary since some people had been saying, "There's no resurrection of the dead" (verse 12). Paul argued that if the dead are not raised, then Christ had not been raised. And if that statement is true, then the apostle's teaching and people's faith in Christ were in vain (verses 14-17).

Although verse 19 begins our lection, it ends the paragraph that began at verse 12. Paul's teaching about the life that believers have in Christ because of his resurrection extended far beyond this mortal life; those who did not believe this were to be "pitied" (verse 19). Most members of the Corinthian church did believe that Christ was raised but viewed his resurrection as a one-time miracle that had no impact on the resurrection of others. For Paul, Christ's resurrection was not an isolated incident. Instead, it was the start of a ripple effect, like throwing a stone in a pond. Because Christ was resurrected, others will also be raised from the dead. In verse 23, he explained that Christ was the first one to be raised, but then "those who belong to Christ" will also be raised "at his coming." His metaphor is one of a harvest of crops, with Christ being "the first fruits of those who have died" (verse 20, NRSV). "Death," Paul asserted, "is the last enemy to be brought to an end" (verse 26).

Luke 24:1-12

The Easter Gospel lection focuses on Luke's account of the women's discovery of the empty tomb. These women, who are not identified by name until verse 10, also witnessed Jesus' crucifixion (23:49) and burial (23:55). "Mary Magdalene, Joanna, Mary the mother of James, and the other women with them" (24:10) went to the tomb on Sunday morning to properly prepare Jesus' body for burial (albeit after the fact). This preparation included washing, anointing with spices, and clothing the body. The stone had already been rolled away, so they entered the tomb immediately and were puzzled to find that the body was gone. Two angelic-looking beings explained to them that Jesus was not here because he had been raised from the dead (verses 4-6). Their explanation quoted Jesus' own words about being handed over, crucified, and raised on the third day. The women then remembered what Jesus had said. In contrast to the other Synoptic Gospel accounts (Matthew 28:7; Mark 16:7) where the one in the tomb told the women to go and tell Jesus' disciples that he had been raised from the dead, the women returned to the disciples without any instructions from the two in "gleaming bright clothing" (verse 4). On their own initiative, the women in Luke's Gospel reported to the disciples what they had witnessed. However, the disciples dismissed the women's report as "nonsense" (verse 11) or "an idle tale" (verse 11, NRSV).

Verse 12 is not included in all translations because scholarly opinion is divided about its authenticity within Luke's Gospel. The CEB, NRSV, NIV, and KJV all include it, so we will explore its meaning. Peter must have taken the women's report more seriously, for he "ran to the tomb" (verse 12) and peered inside. The body was certainly gone; all that remained was "the linen cloth" (verse 12). Peter wondered "what had happened" (verse 12). The fact that the body was missing did not prove that Jesus had been resurrected. Luke's Gospel continues with the encounter of Cleopas and his companion with Jesus on the road to Emmaus and Jesus' post-resurrection appearance to the disciples. Jesus' disciples do come to believe that he is resurrected. Their belief is not based on the empty tomb but on his appearances among them.*

SESSION PLAN

To set the mood for Easter.

Make a graffiti board of Easter traditions

Supplies: Following the Way, large sheets of paper, markers

Greet each other with these historic words: "Christ is risen! Christ is risen indeed! Alleluia!"

Encourage participants to think of Easter traditions that are important to them. They may wish to review the first and last paragraph of the introduction for "A New Day" in *Following the Way* for some ideas. Suggest that participants go to one of the large sheets of paper that you have posted around the room and using one of the markers you have provided draw a symbol or write a few words to identify a tradition that sets the Easter mood for them. These words and symbols are to look like random graffiti. Here are some ideas if prompts are needed: dyed eggs, butterflies as symbols of the Resurrection, new clothing, music such as Handel's "Hallelujah Chorus" or Charles Wesley's "Christ the Lord Is Risen Today," art depicting the Resurrection, sunrise service, Easter Vigil, and Easter baskets.

Take a few moments to look at the graffiti boards to appreciate and comment on the rich traditions that help us to celebrate this most important day in the Christian calendar.

To recognize that God's salvation is for all
(Acts 10:34-43).

A   Imagine Acts 10:34-43

Supplies: Bibles, Following the Way

Invite participants to relax, close their eyes, and try to imagine the scene as you read "No Partiality" in *Following the Way*.

Talk with participants about what they saw, heard, smelled, touched, or tasted as you read.

Choose a volunteer to read Acts 10:34-43, our lection for today in which Peter preaches to Cornelius and his household. Then ask these questions:

1. Had you been Cornelius, what reservations might you, as a Roman military leader, have had in inviting Peter to your home, a preacher of a fringe sect whose leader was crucified by your own government?
2. Had you been Peter, an observant Jew who followed the Jewish Messiah, what reservations would you have had about preaching to Gentiles about Jesus?
3. How did the visions experienced by Cornelius and Peter enable them to bridge the gap between their Jewish and Gentile identities?

4. How might you have felt or reacted had you been among the listeners?
5. What did the listeners learn from this experience?
6. What did Peter learn?

B   Unpack the meaning of the Scripture

Supplies: Bibles, Following the Way

Read or retell the first paragraph of the Bible Background for Acts 10:34-43 to set the stage for today's passage.
Recruit a volunteer to read Acts 10:34-43 and then discuss these questions:
1. What do you learn about how God views all people?
2. What do you learn about Jesus from this passage?
3. What do you learn about Peter?
4. What might Peter's new understanding that God shows no partiality teach the contemporary church?

To confront the reality of death
(1 Corinthians 15:19-26).

A   Clarify views on death

Supplies: Bibles, Following the Way

Select a volunteer to read the portion of "The Death of Death" that begins with "I read" and ends with "fear and dread?" and then ask these questions:
1. Do you agree with Stanley Hauerwas that the avoidance of death at all costs is an integral feature of the American psyche? What evidence can you give to support your answer?
2. What are signs that at least some Americans attempt to live as though they will not die?
Put today's Scripture reading into context by reading or retelling the Bible Background for 1 Corinthians. Then enlist a reader for 1 Corinthians 15:19-26 and discuss these questions:
1. What concerns does the Corinthian church have about death?
2. How are the Corinthians' views similar to and different from those of many Americans?
3. Our writer states, "Hauerwas' point is that Christ's death changes the way we live, not the way we die. We live knowing full well that we will die, but we also live knowing full well that our death is not the end of our story. Death has forever lost its sting because of the cross." How do you think most Americans would respond to this observation? How do you think most Christians would respond?
Provide a few minutes for quiet reflection on this question: Are your views of death more in line with those of most Americans, with those of the

Corinthians who questioned resurrection; or with Hauerwas' point that yes, we will die, but death is not the end of our story because of the cross? Why do you hold your position?

B Recognize that Christ defeated death

Supplies: Bibles, Following the Way, paper, pencils

Choose a volunteer to read 1 Corinthians 15:19-26.

Follow up by asking someone to read from "The Death of Death," beginning with "If you read" and ending with "because of the cross."

Distribute paper and pencils. Read aloud the following information: Paul wrote in 1 Corinthians 15:22 that "in the same way that everyone dies in Adam, so also everyone will be given life in Christ." Yet, we know that most people, including many Christians, try to avoid death at all costs. Write a letter to a loved one explaining your views on the meaning of death. Is it truly the end, or do you expect something else beyond mortal death? Do you believe that Christ has defeated death? How do your beliefs help or hinder your ability to face death?

Call time and encourage several volunteers to read or explain their thoughts.

To affirm that Christ has been raised from the dead and is alive (Luke 24:1-12).

A Dance for joy at the news of resurrection

Supplies: Bibles, Following the Way, recording of "Lord of the Dance" (or other appropriate lively tune) and player

Recommend that participants quickly scan "Lord of the Dance" in *Following the Way*. Point out that the image of the dance is appropriate for conveying our joy in the news of the Resurrection.

Invite those who are able to stand where they can move freely. Indicate that you will read aloud Luke 24:1-12 and at the end of the reading you will immediately start a lively tune. Participants need not "dance" as such but encourage them to move in joyful response to the events of Easter morning.

Read aloud these words from "Lord of the Dance" in *Following the Way* for participants to ponder for a few moments: "Could it be that what matters is conspicuousness? Exuberance? Could it be that a proper response to the amazing grace of Christ's resurrection is to step about in the routine of our living with the grace and lightness of a dancer, and in so doing, to stir up among others the Spirit of the living God?"

Ask: How do you respond to these reflections by the writer?